FLIGHTS FROM FASSBERG

Flights from
FASSBERG

How a
German Town
Built for War
Became a
Beacon of Peace

To Aziz and Sara with best wishes — [signature] 3/22/2022

WOLFGANG W. E. SAMUEL

Colonel, United States Air Force (Ret.)

University Press of Mississippi / Jackson

Willie Morris Books in Memoir and Biography

The University Press of Mississippi is the scholarly publishing agency of the
Mississippi Institutions of Higher Learning: Alcorn State University, Delta
State University, Jackson State University, Mississippi State University,
Mississippi University for Women, Mississippi Valley State University,
University of Mississippi, and University of Southern Mississippi.

www.upress.state.ms.us

The University Press of Mississippi is a member
of the Association of University Presses.

Illustrations courtesy of the author unless otherwise noted

First printing 2021
∞

Library of Congress Control Number 2021930255

Hardback ISBN 978–1-4968–3364–8
Epub single ISBN 978–1-4968–3365–5
Epub institutional ISBN 978–1-4968–3366–2
PDF single ISBN 978–1-4968–3367–9
PDF institutional ISBN 978–1-4968–3363–1

British Library Cataloging-in-Publication Data available

CONTENTS

FOREWORD

As a youngster just turned ten I found myself embroiled in the last throws of a dying Third Reich, losing my home, and barely surviving the bombs and bullets that came along with it. The change from innocent childhood to whatever it was I became thereafter was so drastic that I had little time to absorb it all, much less consider its implications. I reached probably the nadir of my young life when one day my mother's life was nearly terminated by a Russian bullet. Her survival was absolutely miraculous and provided such an uplift to this young boy, that thereafter I felt I could cope with anything that might come my way. I absolutely believed that I owed my mother's life to God's direct intervention.

The immediate years that followed were challenging. Living in the Russian zone of occupation I quickly learned about and experienced the hard fist of totalitarianism. There was the knock on the door at night, always at night, and my grandfather vanished never to be seen again by his family. There was the wrong word said, and my classmates were physically beaten. Only weeks earlier I had been beaten by Hitler Youths in this same town; the same thing continued, just under a different banner. My courageous father came in late 1946 and saved us, fleeing to the British zone of occupation, to a little town called Fassberg. Things were not much different there than in the East when it came to food or anything else that made life livable. But my mother no longer had to worry about getting raped when looking for food for her children, and I again was able to attend a school where they taught things other than propaganda.

Living in abandoned German army barracks in a spontaneously created refugee camp was a dispiriting experience. It took all my strength to make it from one day to the next—until I got angry with myself and remembered that I still had my mother, my Mutti; others didn't. I was alive. I could feel cold and hunger, unlike so many of my young friends who had died and could not feel anything anymore. After I gained that essential insight—called hope—I was able to cope. The little town of Fassberg had experienced almost no damage during the war years. It was an uplifting experience every time I left my barracks behind and I entered this little town of peace and tranquility. I had no idea how it was born, that it was a town built specifically to support an air base created to wage war.

With war at its end, the British occupiers had little use for this air base, and it seemed in late 1947 that it might close—with that, the little town built to support its operation would of course die. But nothing in life is ever absolute, and suddenly friction that developed between former allies became the town's savior. The Berlin airlift of 1948, partially flown out of Fassberg Air Base, assured the little town's survival. Years later, at the height of the Cold War years, Fassberg was an essential air base in the NATO defense structure, and my young son would in fact train there in his A-10 aircraft should Soviet aggression again become physical.

Fassberg is an integral part of my own life, and although the Berlin airlift has been written about by many—the story of Fassberg, one of several airlift bases in 1948, has never really been told from its very beginning in 1933 to the present. And so I chose to do it through the perspective of my own family's experience. I want to thank all who contributed, from the Berlin airlift flyers I interviewed, to the Berlin Airlift Association members who supported me, to the American military policeman who as a young man served at RAF Fassberg, and graciously provided me with all the pictures he took at the time.

He had learned of me from one of my books, and before an untimely
death from cancer, he instructed his wife to forward his pictures to
me. I do not have his name, but I want to honor his memory in this
book. He was as much a part of the Berlin airlift as any flyer, and I
have to thank him and all the others for giving me a life worth living.
Thank you!

FLIGHTS FROM FASSBERG

1

When My World Turned Upside Down

I learned that everything can be taken away from you in a flash of a moment. You need to be very, very grateful for what you have this moment, because that's all you have. You don't have yesterday anymore, and you do not yet have and may never have tomorrow.
—**Christa Glowalla,** from an interview in Wolfgang W. E. Samuel, *The War of Our Childhood*

The morning of January 24, 1945, was just like any other morning for me. I went to school, learned my words and numbers as I was told to, then I couldn't wait to get home and play. Playing with my friends was really all I cared about. On the way home, early that afternoon, we boys strapped our leather satchels to our chests and ran into each other, one trying to knock down the other. And if we should run into girls our age coming out of school—we had separate classes for boys and girls—we would rub snow into their faces and delight when they squealed for us to stop. Once home we built snow forts or had snowball fights, played hide and seek, or whatever game someone came up with—but not war. We didn't play war. Most of our fathers were involved in the war which none of us understood but wished would be over soon. Some of my friends had lost their fathers. They didn't talk about it. But I had noticed that the war we were fighting was not going well. I saw more and more obituaries of young men in our weekly paper, many just teenagers who had died somewhere—they didn't say where. All they said was Ostfront or Westfront or Italy. Few men were around anymore, those who were, were either too old to serve in the military or were missing an arm or a leg or had some other serious war-related wound. I also noticed that on the radio there were no more special announcements celebrating great victories by the Wehrmacht. Instead they seemed to be constantly straightening out their lines, which I figured meant retreat. I had read in our weekly newspaper about atrocities committed by the Russians in East Prussia, and I was worried about my mother Hedy, my Mutti. I wondered how far away from us they might be. And if they got here, what would happen then? My dear Opa Samuel, my dad's father, had come by in December to talk Mutti into staying with him and Oma in Pomerania, but Mutti had laughed it off and Opa, disappointed, took the train home—from Sagan to Berlin, then from Berlin to Stettin, and another train to Schlawe, his hometown. Oma and Opa had a nice house there and I always loved being with them. Opa had served in the Great War, World War I some called it now, and the previous fall, when I was visiting, I found lots of his medals in a drawer. I asked if I could have them. He gave them to me. He didn't care about his medals. So I took them with me when he brought me home to Sagan and traded them at school for some Karl May books, which we were not allowed to have, but we traded them among ourselves anyway. The ones I liked best were the ones about American Indians. But everything good about America was *verboten*, and I talked about the books I read only to my closest friends.

By four o'clock that afternoon it was dark, dark and cold. I briefly thought about my birthday. In a few days I was going to be ten years old. I thought about my friends, and if Mutti had enough flour and things to bake me a cake so I could invite them to my birthday party. Later that evening after dinner an army lieutenant, a friend of Mutti's, came by and wouldn't leave until she had packed three suitcases

My mother Hedy, sister Ingrid, and I in front of our apartment house in Sagan in 1941. I was six years old, Ingrid two. I had not started school yet. Ours was newly built government housing near the air base where my father had been stationed before the war started. The air base added a prisoner of war camp known as *Stalag Luft III*. From our apartment at night I could see the lights of the camp, but as a young boy I had no idea what I was looking at. Photo provided by the author.

for us. Mutti, my little sister Ingrid, and I, and the lieutenant quietly went down the stairs in our apartment house and proceeded to the *Bahnhof*, the train station, where supposedly a train was to arrive later on that night to take us to Berlin, where we would stay with the lieutenant's parents. Frau Hein, who lived in one of the downstairs apartments, was the only one with a telephone. And if she heard and saw us through the peep-hole in her door coming down the stairs carrying suitcases she would surely have called the police, or one of her *Partei* bosses. She always tried to get Mutti to join the *Partei*, but Mutti never did. So we went down the stairs without making any noise. On the way to the train station it didn't dawn on me that I would never be coming back here again, that I would never see my friends again, that I had become a *Fluechtling*, a refugee, one of millions streaming west to escape the advancing Russian armies.

It took Mutti some talking to convince the stationmaster to allow us to buy tickets for Berlin, but in time he relented. The platform was empty when we got there. It was snowing and a cold wind was blowing. The promised train didn't arrive until the following night, and by then hundreds of people filled the platform trying to get on a train which to me looked like it was full already as it pulled into the station. I was cold and exhausted, hadn't eaten or slept since the previous evening. My mom told me to stay with the suitcases and wait for her to call me. I finally heard her voice over the shouting of others trying to get on the train. How she managed to get herself and Ingrid on the train I had no idea. But that was my mom, very innovative and not easily discouraged by anything. She waved at me to bring the suitcases to her. There were too many people in the way, so I took the smallest suitcase and headed for the nearest railroad car, where a friendly man leaning out of a window took the suitcase from me. I got the second, then the third, the largest. By the time I managed to wrestle it up to the man, I heard the stationmaster blow his whistle. And nearly instantly the train shook and began to move out of the station. The doors were jammed with people, dropping away as the train gathered speed. There was no way for me to get on the train that took my mother and sister away, and was leaving me behind. I clearly understood what was happening to me and I was terrified. I wanted to die rather than lose my mom and have no one, no one I could be with. I ran beside the train as it pulled out of the station. I could hear my mom screaming my name, WOLFGANG, WOLFGANG, over and over again. I knew I would never see her or my sister again. And as the end of the platform approached I raised my arms in desperation and called out, "Please, somebody help me, help me." I had no expectation anyone would or could. At the last

moment, people leaning out a window, yanked me off the train platform, through a window and onto the train. I recall the clickety-clack
of the wheels as they passed over the rails, being slammed against
the side of the speeding car, and the darkness of night, and being
pulled slowly, painfully through the train window. I would relive that
experience in my nightmares for many years to come.

Berlin had its own nightmares to live through. At night the Royal
Air Force (RAF) bombers arrived to drop their bombs at random all
over the city. During the day the Americans came with their huge
four-engine bomber fleets. A day after my tenth birthday in February 1945 they attacked with over a thousand bombers, I learned in
later years. The bombs came so close that day, I was sure I was going
to die. We sat in our basement shelter, women and children and a
few old men, awaiting death. As the bomb explosions came closer
and closer I could feel the floor beneath me shake, the whitewash
came off the walls, and it was hard to breathe. I could not take this
much longer; I knew that, just sitting there waiting to die. No one
screamed, no one did anything, except hold something over their
mouths and noses to breathe. I didn't die that day, or on other days,
but the terror of those raids, impossible to describe in mere words,
left its mark on me and would not diminish for many years to come.
To hear the wail of a siren, in future years, would take me back to
those terrible days and nights, fill me with fear which would take
over my body and nearly paralyze me at times. In early March our
friendly hosts encouraged us to leave for a safer place, and we took
a train north, to the little country town of Strasburg, where both my
mother and I were born. We stayed with my grandparents Grapentin,
who, unlike my Oma and Opa Samuel, were very poor people, who
lived in a two-room ground-level apartment, with an outhouse for
a toilet, and no running water. We made do, but soon the Russian
army launched its last major attack to bring the war to an end. My
grandparents, Mutti's parents, believed to the very end that the great
Fuehrer, our leader, would somehow turn everything around and

everything would turn out well. But that was not to be. Even I as a ten-year-old understood that.

One night it was our turn to pick things up again and flee west. My grandfather had been drafted into the *Volkssturm*, a militia of the very old and very young. We packed our things and headed up the street to the main road by the market square. My mom had come down with the flu and was feeling bad, yet she dressed in her finest. When my grandmother questioned her, she replied, "Mutti, we can't make it on our own. Someone has to pick us up and take us along. Do you think they will stop for a frumpy looking woman?" So my mother dressed like she was going to a dinner party. She stood by the side of the road waving her arms to get a German army truck or whatever to pick us up and take us along. The miracle happened when a disciplined unit of military police in horse-drawn wagons came by—and one of them stopped and took us along. The days that followed were days of horror. We were strafed by Russian fighters, not hitting our wagons, but killing others all around us. A field of dead would recur in my postwar dreams over and over again, and they looked at me with their dead eyes asking why I was not one of them. I always woke screaming, sitting straight up in bed, bathed in sweat and scared beyond belief. The nightmares lasted well into my forties, then finally the terror waned and released me to sleep through the night. The German soldiers we were fleeing with were adept at killing Russian tanks which came close to us, but they couldn't do anything about the artillery and rocket attacks. A unit of *Waffen-SS* soldiers attempted to stop us, to make a last stand with them. Our soldiers refused, there were more of them than there were of the SS, and we went on heading west—to surrender to the Americans or the British.

On a beautiful late April day it happened. Our column of nearly a hundred horse-drawn wagons stopped. They had traveled in three separate columns and combined when it became clear they were close to British and American lines. On the lead wagon they affixed a white flag on one side—a bed sheet—and an American flag on the other side, and we surrendered peacefully to men of the 7th Armored Division and the 82nd Airborne, I learned in later years. We ended up in a makeshift camp of refugees. There was little water; trenches served as toilets, or the open fields. Cholera soon broke out, killing boys and girls I had befriended. There was no food other than what we had brought along. We were fortunate that we had inherited the supply wagon of the army unit we had fled with. Mom shared things with others, and soon it was all gone. One day an American soldier hailed me. He had a submachine gun slung over his shoulder. I didn't move. He understood the reason for my hesitation, removed the gun from his shoulder, took out the magazine and showed me he only had one bullet in it—he wasn't going to shoot me. I went over to him and in his way he made me understand that they, the Americans, would move out during the night, and to tell everyone. Then he pulled a flat stick out of his pocket and shoved it into his mouth and started chewing, smiling all the while. He gave me one like it, and I started chewing. It tasted good—it was chewing gum I later learned. Never heard of it before, and couldn't quite figure out why I needed something to chew. I soon spit it out. He shook his head, still smiling. Took his gum out of his mouth, rolled it into a ball and put it behind his ear, he had taken off his helmet. Then he put it back into his mouth, chewing vigorously. I guess he was trying to tell me that one could chew this thing forever and ever. I never forgot that American soldier, and his generosity and kindness. It was May, the war was over, and that night the American tanks left, heading west.

We ended up in an abandoned Hitler Youth barracks, with other refugees. The Russians soon came and made their presence known, drinking and raping. Only their officers came; the enlisted men were kept in their camps. Hedy resisted being raped and was shot by an enraged Russian officer. The bullet entered near her jugular vein, and exited within a millimeter of her spine. After a lengthy period of recovery, we returned to Strasburg, where we had started our odyssey, hoping Opa, Hedy's father, had survived the end. He had, only to be imprisoned by German communists for a minor infraction. We later learned that he was beaten to death—not by Russians, but by German communists who ran things in the Russian zone of occupation for the Russian occupiers. I learned little in school, once I entered. Everything came down to propaganda, telling us youngsters how wonderful our new world was going to be and how awful everything was that came before. The only problem was, in this world of ours, there was not much to eat, few places to live, and nothing of value to learn. Mutti, Ingrid, and I were still refugees, outsiders. The winter of '45 was brutal. I had little to wear, having outgrown most of my things. A seamstress made me a pair of pants and a jacket out of army tent material—which offered no warmth, but was good at keeping out the rain. I hoped my father would show up to get us out of our misery—and to my great surprise, one day in the late fall of 1946, he did just that.

Willie, my dad, had served in the Luftwaffe and when captured by Patton's troops served some time as a prisoner of war, but soon was released. He returned to his last base of assignment—Fassberg. I had no idea where Fassberg was, since I had never been able to find the place on a map. All I knew was that it was somewhere near Hannover in the Lueneburg Heath. He found a couple of rooms in an abandoned army barracks, as did many other refugees, soon filling the cluster of barracks to capacity. Then he looked for his parents, my grandparents, assuming that they, along with others, had been expelled from Pomerania, an area that had been transferred from Germany to Poland. He was in luck and found Oma and Opa Samuel in a refugee camp in Schleswig-Holstein. He brought them down to the makeshift refugee camp where he had managed to hold on to the two rooms. My grandfather was a man of integrity and honor, and he passed his passions on to me through deed and word. He found some work on a nearby potato farm and one of the first things he managed to do was to have them drill a well in the center of the camp and install a water pump. A simple hand-operated pump. The water supply for the barracks compound when it was still a German army facility came from the nearby Trauen rocket research center, just up the road, adjacent to the Fassberg *Flugplatz*, the military airfield. The research center was shut down after war's end, and the water stopped flowing. Once refugees moved into the now abandoned army barracks, water was supplied from the nearby potato farm about twice a week by a team of horses, which pulled a water wagon into the middle of the compound. People then came running out to fill their cans and buckets. Water was a precious commodity and getting a pump installed made it available to everyone whenever they needed water. The pump served a population of well over a hundred people. Then, by late fall of 1946, my father figured that just maybe we would be staying in Strasburg, Hedy's hometown, since he hadn't been able to locate us anywhere else. So, here he was; he had found us and come to take us back.

Hedy and Willie were estranged because of his many affairs with other women, and I wasn't sure if my mother was going to go along with her husband's wishes and follow him to the Fassberg area. Their minds were made up for them by circumstances. An informer in the house where we lived, a former *Gasthaus*, reported Willie's arrival to the police, and a friend of Mutti's who worked the telephone exchange in Strasburg for the authorities told her that she had overheard telephone discussions that Willie, a former Luftwaffe officer, was to be arrested soon, with destination Siberia. Not only that, the following afternoon a young girl appeared. I still recall her vividly standing in the doorway talking to my mother. She stood there fidgeting, uneasy, telling my mother that her father had told her to tell her that she and Willie should take a train west or my father would be arrested later that night. Arrests were always made at night. My grandfather was arrested at night, and everyone who disappeared without ever being seen again always vanished at night. "There is a train leaving this evening," she said, "and if you are not on it, your husband Willie will be arrested before the night is over." The girl was the daughter of a police officer, who had sent her at the risk of his own life should any of his fellow officers find out what he had done. We left Ingrid behind. Winter had set in, so we grabbed a minimum of possessions and took the train to freedom, to the West, the British zone of occupation. It was a slow journey to Wittenberge, near the Russian zonal border. As we tried to cross the border on foot, East German police arrested us and took us to their station. They were former Wehrmacht soldiers and were willing to help us in our endeavor to cross over to the other side once they learned that my father had been a Luftwaffe officer.

The commander of the station told my father the schedule of the Russian patrols, and we set off into the unknown. A blizzard had developed in the meantime and was driving snow before it into our faces. I was wearing my camouflage suit, it was all I had. It provided no warmth. Why I didn't die of exposure that day I don't know, but when we reached a small railroad station on the other side, I was at the end of my strength and bleeding severely from my thighs which had been rubbed raw by the stiff material of my pants. I recall lying in front of a pot-bellied wood stove and screaming in agony as my limbs thawed out. Many years later, my son Charles invited me to take a trip replicating our route of flight at the time. The rail station was still there, but the rail line was no longer in use. When I knocked, a woman opened the door and readily opened up the area that once had been the waiting room. The pot-bellied stove was still there. So were the memories; they are there for life.

The train ride took us to Uelzen, then to Munster-Lager, a small army garrison town. Munster-Lager had been an army training camp since the Kaiser's days, and my grandfather Samuel had trained troops there from 1904 to 1908 for the Herero uprising in German Southwest Africa, now Namibia. From Munster-Lager eventually we took a train to the small village of Trauen—Trauen, adjacent to the Fassberg Air Base, I was to learn, had been a V2 rocket research center, a *Raketenversuchsanstalt*. Mutti and I crowded around my father on the windswept platform at the Trauen station. He pointed up a road, paved with square granite stones, leading to the main entrance of the research center. "There are the barracks," he said. "We are home." About half a kilometer up the road, adjacent to a pine forest, stood several former Wehrmacht barracks. To the right of the forest were open fields. I could make out the shapes of what seemed like hundreds of military aircraft. "They are old German bombers," my dad explained to me, anticipating my question. "We are at the outside perimeter of what once was the Fassberg *Flugplatz.*" From a distance the planes looked alive to me, like they were ready to start their engines and taxi out onto a runway to take off for some distant war. There was no war anymore, and I was glad it was over.

We walked quietly for the remainder of the way. When dad opened the door to what was to be our home, there stood my grandmother Samuel. Her eyes lit up as she saw us, and the tears rolled down her hollow cheeks. Her gnarled, rheumatic hands held an aluminum pot she was just taking off a cast-iron stove. She put down the pot carefully and called to my grandfather who was in the back room, "Come quickly, the children are here." I slept really well that night, no nightmares. Over the following weeks I had ample opportunity to get familiar with my new surroundings. There were three barracks in our compound, all filled with *Fluechtlinge*, refugees, mostly from the East—East Prussia, Silesia, like myself, or Pomerania. There was also a Dutch family living in one of the barracks. Rumor had it they had been German-friendly during the war, and left when the German army moved out. The barracks were arranged in a U shape. At the open end of the U was a smaller barrack which contained two rows of six seats opposite of each other, with two private latrines at one end—I presume they were for the senior sergeants, when the compound was still military. Our apartment, which now housed five, consisted of two rooms. The front room was the kitchen and living area, the back room held our beds and served as a storage area. All the furniture was used or improvised. Life was very basic—all that mattered was to have a roof over our heads, a bed, in my case a sack filled with straw, wood for cooking and heating, and some food of whatever kind. Rooms were divided by thin walls of pine board. I quickly learned there were few secrets in the barracks, because anything said above a whisper was overheard by someone and quickly became common knowledge. You would hear your neighbors cough, turn in their bed, or make love. There was no privacy.

Every workday morning at about seven, a Royal Air Force truck from Fassberg Air Base would pull into the compound and sit there for about ten minutes by the water pump idling, spewing foul-smelling exhaust fumes. The truck picked up men and women who were fortunate enough to have found work at the air base. The truck brought them back at about five in the afternoon. Usually the women sat on the folding benches in back of the truck and the men stood, holding on to the metal frame that held the tarpaulin which covered the truck bed. When they returned in the evening, some brought back food given to them by English families as payment for some service they had provided. One especially prized item was the English bread—white, with a brown crust on top, baked in a pan that made the bread look like a cake, and to us it was as good or better. Some fortunate ones brought back English coffee, real coffee made from coffee beans, not the German ersatz coffee made from roasted barley, called *Katreiner*. Oh, the smell of real coffee was precious to me. In my world most of the smells I recalled had been bad, some even ugly, terrifying. English coffee smelled like a breath from heaven. Smells colored my world—the smell of gunpowder, of burning rubber and uniforms, the stench of burning human flesh or that of our camp latrine. The best smell though by far for me was the smell of a bar of Palmolive soap my father had on our washbasin. A clean smell. It drove out of my mind the smells of burning people and gunpowder.

Most of the women were employed as maids in the households of English officers or senior sergeants in Fassberg. Others worked in the canteen, the officers' mess, or as cleaning women in offices or

My sister Ingrid, age eight, standing in front of our barracks surrounded by children of the Trauen refugee camp, with Teddy our faithful spitz. Teddy liked roaming in the nearby woods; one day he didn't come home. We never saw Teddy again and missed him greatly. Photo provided by the author.

maintenance shops. The men worked in the motor pool, as carpenters and electricians, and in other skilled trades the English occupiers had a need for. My father had found work in Munster-Lager, the large army military training area, as an electrician with a British army searchlight battery. There was no truck to pick him up, so he walked the eight kilometers to Munster-Lager each day. On occasion he would stay there overnight. He too brought home English bread and coffee, and now and then English cigarettes, much better than anything German, which he traded on the black market for food.

As the December days passed my mother became more and more restless. Just before Christmas she persuaded my sixty-six-year-old grandfather to return with her to the Russian zone to get Ingrid. My grandfather's willingness to join Mutti in this obviously hazardous venture didn't surprise me. I had never known him to be anything but resolute and courageous. He probably saw this rescue as a duty, if not a welcome opportunity to do something meaningful. On December 23, 1946, the two set off on their perilous journey. I was uneasy, not sure if I would ever see them again. January proved to be bitter cold. The frigid winds swept the snow before them, piling it into high drifts around the barracks. My father thought it was high time for me to get back into school. I had had no meaningful schooling since January 1945 when we fled Sagan for Berlin. I knew my education was seriously flawed, and going to the village school in Trauen would probably doom me forever. My father quieted my fears. He thought he could enroll me in a much better school in Fassberg. He knew the school's principal, Herr Soffner, and thought he could get him to make an exception and allow me to attend school there. He and Herr Soffner talked when we met in early February. Herr Soffner asked me how old I was. "Twelve. I just turned twelve a few days ago," I told him. "Well, then you should be in the sixth grade." He bade my father farewell, took me by the shoulders, and led me to my classroom. My joy was tempered by the expressionless faces looking at me from behind their desks.

Every day I walked the four kilometers or more from the barracks to my new school in Fassberg. I liked being back in school where they taught real academic subjects, not political propaganda. I couldn't take English, although I wanted to. The English teacher thought her class was too far along and I wouldn't be able to catch up. I realized that I was far behind my classmates in my education. I decided to do the best I could. My first weeks were a period of adjustment and making new friends. I was made acutely aware that I was an outsider, a refugee from the East, a *Fluechtling*. As a result I got into frequent fights. I was different, and being different in Germany meant being an outsider. No one invited me to play or to come to anything such as a birthday party. In spite of it all, I liked Fassberg. It was whole and clean, with few reminders of war. Every day as I left the squalor and poverty of the barracks behind and came closer to Fassberg, a load

My classroom was behind the main building, a converted storage room. We played schoolyard soccer right here in front by the fence using old tennis balls or anything round. The girls spent their classroom breaks on the other side; we didn't mix. Photo provided by the author.

lifted off my shoulders. Fassberg was tranquil and orderly in contrast to my world of stress and deprivation. Fassberg became a place of solace, healing, and peace for me. When I stepped out of the forest onto the paved sidewalks and walked through the English housing area, I began to feel clean and free, maybe, just maybe, somewhere in the distant future there would be a better life for me. I refused to feel sorry for myself.

Every Monday, Wednesday, and Friday, a wonderful event occurred at school. A group of volunteer women served us students a cup of hot chocolate and a handful of peanuts. The peanuts were delicious. I didn't know what they were, if they grew on a tree, bush, or some other plants. I sipped the hot chocolate while it was still hot enough to burn my tongue. I was often very cold when I arrived at school, because I had to walk so far in my thin clothes and plastic

My Oma Grapentin, a simple farm woman. She boiled water in a tin can over an open fire before allowing Ingrid or me to drink it when we were in our first refugee camp in May 1945—saving us from contracting cholera and dying like so many other children did. Photo provided by the author.

shoes. I didn't miss a Monday, Wednesday, or Friday ever. I didn't miss any school days. Each school day was precious to me. I came down with the flu in the winter of 1947–1948. I dragged myself to school every day so as not to miss the peanuts and hot chocolate. Often I went to school without having had breakfast of any kind. Our classes started at eight o'clock in the morning and ended at one in the afternoon. By the time I walked home it was two or later before I had anything to eat. I didn't mind. I had gotten used to doing without food. But I couldn't do without hope. Fassberg and my school gave me hope for a better future.

In the meantime my mother and Opa Samuel had safely returned from their perilous journey to the Russian zone of occupation, bringing my little sister Ingrid and my cousin Vera, who was seventeen years old. Both Vera and Marie, her mother, as the war ended in

April 1945, had been raped by Russian officers for days on end. Marie died of typhus fever, and Hedy believed she owed it to her deceased sister to give Vera the opportunity at a better life. Oma Grapentin, Hedy's mom, decided to remain behind. No one had told her how my grandfather had died, so she stayed with my uncle Ernst, Mutti's younger brother, waiting for her beloved husband to return, a return that was never going to happen.

2

A Town Built for War

In mid-September appeared a man from Berlin to purchase land from heath farmers. He negotiated for a 'third' party, which was no further identified in the purchase contracts.
—**Hans Staerk**, *Fassberg*

The year 1933 was to be a watershed year not only for Germany, but for the world as a whole. The fledgling German Weimar Republic was about to fail, with the rest of the world taking little notice. An extreme right wing party, the NSDAP (*Nationale Socialistische Deutsche Arbeiter Partei*, commonly referred to in later years as NAZIS), led by an Austrian, a naturalized German citizen, Adolf Hitler, took control when its leader was appointed chancellor on January 30, 1933, by ailing President von Hindenburg. Within the next thirty days Hitler tightened his grip on the nation. The Reichstag, the parliament building in Berlin went up in flames, emergency decrees were issued suspending civil liberties, and Hitler's private army, the SA, *Sturmabteilung*, took over terrorizing any opposition. Within days Germany transitioned from its attempt to be a representative republic to dictatorship.

The peace treaty of Versailles precluded Germany from creating an air force and limited the German army to a maximum of 100,000

men. Such provisions didn't keep German planners from circum-
venting the treaty limitations, and as early as 1924 ten flying schools
were established, ostensibly for the training of those who viewed flying as a sport. The German navy established similar training schools,
and of course civil aviation, which began to develop in earnest about
this time, required similar training opportunities. To provide realistic
military-type aviation training, in 1924, a secret training center was
opened as well in Lipetsk, Russia. This secret air base arrangement
allowed for the testing of military aircraft and the training of future
fighter pilots and observers. This arrangement was terminated in
1933, when Hitler, a fervent anticommunist, assumed power. So, on
February 2, 1933, two years to the day before I was born, Hermann
Goering was put in charge of German aviation, military and civil.
His task was to develop a powerful Luftwaffe as quickly as possible
and on May 15, 1933 he created the *Reichsluftfahrtministerium*, better
known by its acronym of RLM. All future planning for the still secret
Luftwaffe was done by the RLM.

In August 1933 the RLM moved out smartly and ordered the
construction of several air bases, including four training bases, one
of which was to be named Fassberg, in the Lueneburg Heath. All
of the new air bases carried unrevealing cover names. In the case
of Fassberg, which would not appear on any maps until after war's
end, the airfield was named *Hanseatischefliegerschule Fassberg E.V.*, a
cover name to hide its planned military uses. Fassberg was the name
of a nearby hill of less than three hundred feet elevation and was as
good a name as any. In World War II the small hillside was bombed
several times by the Royal Air Force, while the base itself received
little damage. The Nazis moved fast. They started buying up land for
the new base that September. If you chose not to sell your land to the
unnamed buyer, the German state would just take it. A rail connection to the future air base was promptly built, and by that November
work began in earnest on the airfield and the town which was to
house the people who operated and supported the airfield. In 1933

there was no dearth of laborers for such an undertaking. Germany was going through a major economic crisis, as was the rest of the world, and Hitler promised to put everyone to work, which he did by building major four-lane, limited-access highways, *Autobahnen*, and military bases such as the Fassberg airfield,

Another similar base for future fighter operations was being built near the county seat of Celle, very near the planned town and air base of Fassberg. Much of the work to build these two air bases was done with pick and shovel, and every man who wanted a job suddenly had one. Pay was low but enough to feed their families. In addition, Hitler initiated the building of the famed *Volkswagen*, the People's Car. A car for every German family lay in the future, and he was ostensibly building the roads to accommodate them. No mention was made of the Autobahn's real purpose, to quickly move troops across Germany once war started. Then a final and very important addition was being developed for Germany's new leader to communicate with his people—the *Volksempfaenger*. Like the *Volkswagen*, the People's Car, here came the *Volksemphaenger*, the People's Radio. It was a very simple radio, cheap, so even the lowest paid worker could afford one—a status symbol which both of my grandparents owned. And when Hitler gave one of his many rousing speeches, people sat by their *Volksemphaengers*, mesmerized, listening intently, not to miss a word he said. Autobahns, Volkswagens, and the Peoples' Radios coupled to high unemployment, a post–World War I residue of feelings of "having been stabbed in the back," and a polarized and fractured political establishment was a dictator's recipe for success.

The large number of workers required for the construction of Fassberg Air Base, and the adjacent town to accommodate all of those who would operate such a facility, were housed in nearby villages and towns, and each morning and evening were transported by rail to and from the construction site. Some who could not find accommodations were put up in hastily built barracks. The first buildings completed were three very large aircraft hangars.

Come April 1934, a combat wing, Kampfgeschwader 154, KG 154, was activated with three squadrons. The first aircraft arrived the following month. Air crews began to train on aircraft such as the Arado 66 and Heinkel 45, biplanes, and the Heinkel 46. The runways were dirt, not concrete or asphalt, and fit in with the general theme of providing natural camouflage as much as possible. Both the town of Fassberg and base facilities were built into the forest to provide the intended camouflage, which apparently worked well during the coming war years. In addition, a fake airfield was built nearby with grass runways, including landing lights, a frequent target for British night fighters during the later war years. As a result of these very well planned camouflage efforts, the actual air base was never targeted. As flying activity picked up, an unpleasant discovery was made—the Lueneburg Heath in general is a very sandy place and as aircraft powered up their engines they soon became clogged with dust and sand. The first attempt at a solution to the problem was to plant grass, which improved things, but didn't solve the problem. Especially after a soaking rain the runways were for all practical purposes unusable. If a pilot decided to land anyway, the result was predictably unfavorable; if lucky, he and his crew survived. Many didn't. To the end of the war Fassberg airfield never got a hard-surface concrete runway. They just made do.

In his self-published book *Fassberg* (1971), Hans Staerk points out that German youngsters were as enthusiastic about flying as were their American counterparts. The rush by Goering to quickly create a substantially sized air force starting in 1933 led to many accidents. Lack of experience and excessive enthusiasm by trainees led many youngsters to take chances they were not prepared to deal with. Between June and December 1935, on average, forty-eight aircraft crashed monthly with the loss of twelve pilots. The accident rate came perilously close to endangering the entire air force building program. In those days one pilot would tell another just before take-off, "Hals und Beinbruch," literally translated as 'Break your neck and legs,'

One of three very large aircraft hangars under construction in 1933. Note the control tower at the far end of the hangar under construction. The hangars all had flat roofs, to blend into the environment as much as possible. Construction methods were rudimentary including horse-drawn freight trolleys, and pick and shovel. Photo courtesy of the Fassberg Airlift Museum.

which usually happened when you crashed your aircraft while executing a maneuver badly or on landing, when many of these accidents occurred, particularly on Fassberg's sandy or water-logged runways.

By late summer 1935 Fassberg Air Base was nearly finished with eight large hangars, three unpaved runways and associated taxiways, a quite impressive *Offizierskasino* (officers' club), maintenance facilities, and so on. All that remained to be done was to finish the on-base heated swimming pool, the town church which was intended to serve both principal religious denominations—Protestant and Catholic—and a row of shops. That activity was completed two years later.

As for the young flyers who had joined the secretive Luftwaffe, once ordered to report for duty at Fassberg, they had difficulty finding the air base. No one seemed to know where Fassberg was. Somewhere near Celle or Soltau was the usual response. The

The church was adjacent to my school and to the small shopping area and was one of the last structures completed in 1938, along with the school. Few services were available in Fassberg—no railroad station, no tailor shop, no hotel, no restaurant, nor movie theater. Photo courtesy of the Fassberg Airlift Museum.

nascent Luftwaffe was in fact an illegal organization under the terms of the Versailles treaty, and its members, like my father, wore civilian clothes when reporting for duty. My father Willie, once he finished high school in 1929, at age twenty, had applied for a visa to emigrate to the United States. An uncle had found him a job in an automobile factory in Detroit, a prerequisite at the time for immigrants. Being German he was turned down for an immigration visa. However, a thorough American consulate employee looked at his application and told him that he was actually Polish, to my father's great surprise, and was eligible for a visa reserved for immigrants to the United States from Poland. He was born in Gnesen, a small garrison town in West Prussia, where my grandfather at the time of my father's birth served as a reservist in Dragoner Regiment 12. Gnesen and surrounding areas were ceded to the newly resurrected country of Poland, and the Versailles treaty provided for Poland to have access to the Baltic Sea; ergo a corridor was carved out of the former German Reich between East Prussia and Pomerania and assigned to Poland to provide that essential access to the Baltic Sea. My father's application to emigrate to the United States was approved once he was declared to be Polish.

Of course my grandmother Anna was distraught over her only son's decision to leave for a foreign country. Would she ever see him again? She spent much of her time in tears and persuaded Willie to apply to join the 100,000-man army Germany was allowed to have. Times being hard, acceptance into the army was much sought after, because it provided a sure and steady income, something highly valued by young women looking for a husband. Willie's visa to the United States and his acceptance into the army came through at about the same time—and Anna persuaded her son to stay home, rather than go to a distant foreign land. Had he gone to America, as planned, my father would most likely have worn an American uniform during the war. But listening to my grandmother, he didn't go and so he wore a German uniform.

Willie was originally assigned to Reiter Regiment 6, von Arnim, named after a German nobleman, stationed in Pasewalk, near Strasburg, where he eventually would meet my mother. He joined the newly formed and secretive Luftwaffe in 1933. On March 1, 1935, the Luftwaffe went public, its members now could wear Luftwaffe uniforms, and Fassberg became Fliegerhorst Fassberg, dropping the fanciful name of Hanseatischefliegerschule. The Luftwaffe of 1935 consisted of around 900 officers, many World War I veterans among them, and 10,000 men with a total assignment of around 2,500 aircraft, most of them training related and of dated designs. And the wing assigned to Fassberg Air Base, Kampfgeschwader KG 154, was named Boelcke, after the World War I fighter pilot Hauptmann

Oswald Boelcke, a tactical genius with forty victories, who was killed in 1916 in a midair collision.

In 1935 Hitler made his first significant moves. In a plebiscite that January in the coal-rich Saarland, administered by the League of Nations, voters overwhelmingly opted for reunion with Germany. The Saar was returned to German control on March 1. With such encouragement Hitler promptly denounced the terms of the hated Versailles treaty, reinstated conscription, expanded the size of the army, and casually revealed the existence of the Luftwaffe to the visiting British foreign secretary, Sir John Simon, by stating, "We have already reached parity with Britain." Gutsy, but certainly an overstatement. Ten months later, in March 1936, Hitler makes his first overt move by occupying the demilitarized Rheinland. Fassberg, a training base, was anything but ready to support such an action. France and Great Britain did nothing. The time to act and to stop Hitler was passing swiftly.

While construction of air base facilities proceeded pretty much as planned, the building of a small town to support those who were to run the air base proceeded at a somewhat slower pace. Housing was built in three distinct and separate developments—the Red, the White, and the Gray *Siedlung*. The White housing development was finished first in 1936 and was for ordinary workers. The houses were not brick, but built of limestone covered with plaster. The rooms were very basic and small, and there was only a very small cellar, important to store coal, potatoes, and so on. The cellar space was deemed inadequate to serve as an air raid shelter, so several very basic shelters were built in this section of Fassberg. The Red housing development was intended for officers and higher-ranking civil servants, including some single homes, commanders' houses, with terraces and large enough for entertainment. Those houses in the Red *Siedlung* had full basements, a full bath, flush toilets, and central heating, instead of the coal or wood-fired ovens provided in the workers' homes, who did not have flush toilets but septic tanks. The

My father Willie in his new Luftwaffe uniform in the spring of 1935 holding his newborn son, Wolfgang. I was born in February. On March 1 the Luftwaffe dropped its
pretenses and went public. I presume Willie was very proud to hold his newborn and
wear his new uniform all at the same time. Photo provided by the author.

The Hermann Goering *Wache*, main entrance to the Fassberg Air Base, in 1935, with
a soldier posting guard. Fassberg's main road, referred to locally as the *Betonstrasse*
(concrete road), led directly into the air base. In those days there was very little traffic
of any kind, something that would change significantly in years to come. Today it is
known as the *Hauptwache*, the principal entrance to the airfield. Photo courtesy of the
Fassberg Airlift Museum.

Bruce, a military police dog, in 1949, sitting on the hood of his handler's jeep in front of the planned *Hauptwache*, main entrance, to Fassberg Air Base, which served as the military police headquarters during the Berlin airlift. Above the ornate entrance to the airfield, which was never used as such, 1933–35 is displayed in large letters. Photo provided by the author.

Red housing area was connected to the sewer system of the air base, being adjacent to it. The Gray *Siedlung* was for sergeants and lower-ranking civil servants, and its houses were somewhat larger than the houses in the White development. Only the Red housing development, built of brick, included full bathrooms with tubs, all the others had no more than a washbasin, and for baths every German family owned a zinc tub which was filled with hot water. The entire process, more or less private, usually took place once a week in the kitchen.

The hurried pace of building both the air base and the town resulted in some issues, many of which would never be adequately resolved. The first issue had to do with the sandy soil of the region and swampy areas, which were not taken into account when the air base layout was decided. The main entrance to the base, the *Hauptwache*, was built in the style of the Hitler era with massive columns in front of the building to impress. It turned out its location was not a good choice, because the sandy soil would not support the concrete road planned to lead into it. The principal entrance to the air base to this day, was initially planned to be no more than a side entrance to the air base.

A two-lane concrete road, *Grosse Horststrasse*, initially named after Adolf Hitler, was built to provide access to the air base and town. The town essentially was then built around this road. As for shopping, very little was provided. Located right across from the schoolhouse was a bakery, a butcher shop, and a few other small shops—the bare minimum needed. A hotel or a restaurant was not in the plans. There was no movie theater, other than the one on the air base itself, and no facilities for social events, music, or whatever made a town livable. For all of these things you had to go somewhere else. Most German towns had a central square, a marketplace, where farmers could set up stands to sell their product, where towns held their festivals, and so on. Fassberg did not have such a square. The town center as such was the school, the church, and the shopping area, all of which were located in close proximity to each other. It was a town built for war, and the usual amenities provided by a town for its citizens apparently were considered superfluous by the planners.

After only three years of frenzied activity both the air base and the town of Fassberg were essentially finished. The town accommodated about 700 people, another 1,600 or so lived on the air base. According to Staerk, "As of 1938 there were two small grocery stores in Fassberg, two bakeries, one butcher shop and two barbershops. There was no carpenter, no painter, no electrician, nor tailor to find in Fassberg. One could hardly buy anything." The church and schoolhouse were finished in 1938, with the school designed to accommodate about 130 students. By the time I entered the school in 1947 the student population significantly exceeded that number, and my classroom was a basement room that had been converted to accommodate my class.

Although railroad tracks were laid to run into the airfield, Fassberg itself did not have a train station. With minor exceptions, no one

One of two barbershops in Fassberg serving both men and women. Located in a private residence, this shop is where I went to have my hair cut in 1948. Photo provided by the author.

owned a car or truck in those days, so to catch a train from the nearby village of Unterluess one had to take a bus, which people didn't mind doing. It only cost 15 pfennig for a one-way ride. Once a week a bus ran to the nearby town of Celle, and once a month a bus drove as far as Hannover, a substantially sized city, where in years to come I would enter an apprenticeship as a baker after finishing the eighth grade in Fassberg. Social life in Fassberg was indeed limited, but people made do.

As for the air base, in prewar days it was essentially a training center using Dornier 17 and 23 aircraft, Junkers 52 transports, and Heinkel 111 bombers. In 1937 Professor Heinrich Focke, of Focke-Wulf 190 fighter fame in later years, who taught, worked, and lived in Bremen, designed and constructed the first helicopter, an effort deemed impossible by many at the time. He did it by fitting rotors, vertically mounted to an aircraft fuselage "enabling the machine to rise vertically from the ground, remain stationary in midair, and fly backward and forward," recalled Hanna Reitsch, one of Germany's most famous and accomplished test pilots, in her autobiography

Flying Is My Life. "The famous American flyer, Colonel Charles A. Lindbergh, came on a visit to Germany, it fell to me to demonstrate the helicopter to him in Bremen. Lindbergh was so impressed that he called the helicopter the most striking aeronautical development he had ever seen." In late 1937 Hanna was attempting to set a world distance record by flying the Focke-Wulf 61 *Hubschrauber*, helicopter, from Bremen to Berlin. Fassberg airfield was not on her flight plan, however, en route to Berlin the oil overheated and she had firm instructions to land immediately if that should happen. She landed in Fassberg. According to Staerk, Reitsch landed in the backyard of a creamery, scaring the daylights out of the workers, who upon seeing such a strange contraption ran off screaming. However, once she shut down the engine and out stepped a young woman, the terrified creamery workers returned and were overjoyed to meet Hanna, once they learned who she was. The creamery had a telephone and Hanna was able to contact Professor Heinrich Focke in Bremen, which wasn't that far from Fassberg, who quickly brought in some mechanics to get her aircraft air worthy again. She then set a world distance record from Fassberg to Berlin. There were no other helicopters flying at the time, so every flight in a sense was indeed a world record. So Fassberg airfield, its location still not recorded on maps, enjoyed a fleeting moment of fame.

In March 1938 aircraft from Fassberg airfield flew their first operational missions in support of the Anschluss of Austria as a German province—renamed the Ostmark. Colonel Anton Heidenreich, whose son was to be a classmate of mine in 1947 when I entered school in Fassberg, had assumed command of the Kampffliegerschule 2, Combat Flight Training School 2, and was ordered to use some of his Ju 52 transport trainers to drop propaganda leaflets over various towns in Austria in support of the takeover of the country by the German army. It was a fairly benign mission, somewhat complicated by blizzard conditions in various areas over Austria, and of course the Ju 52 pilots were still in flight training with little flying experience. Upon

Unterluess was a village rail station, not much different from the tiny station in the village of Trauen. The trains that came here offered no modern comforts—hard wooden benches were the rule. Photo provided by the author.

their return to Fassberg airfield, Colonel Heidenreich and his student pilots celebrated their achievement in a quickly organized dinner party in the newly constructed *Offizierskasino*, officers club. Also present at this dinner was the director of the Trauen *Raketenversuchsanstalt*, rocket test center, Dr. Eugen Saenger. The Trauen rocket test center was located adjacent to the Fassberg airfield and was part of the Voelkenrode/Brunswick research center, the exploitation of which by Colonel Donald Putt in April 1945 would have a powerful effect on aeronautical developments in the United States. See my book *American Raiders* for details on the 1945 capture and exploitation of the Voelkenrode research center. The Trauen research and test center provided the space for Voelkenrode directed large-scale rocket experimentation, space that was not available in Voelkenrode. At the time the Trauen Center was a highly secretive and closely guarded facility.

Heinkel 111 (He 111) and Junkers 88 (Ju 88) bombers, many only temporarily based at Fassberg Air Base, participated in the occupation of Denmark and the attack on Norway, and in air attacks on Holland in April 1940. Colonel Martin Fiebig, the commander of the 4th Combat Wing, Kampfgeschwader 4, then based in Fassberg, led an attack of He 111 aircraft on targets in Holland and was shot down by Dutch fighters as he made his approach to his target coming in from the water side, the North Sea. He briefly became a prisoner of war and returned to Fassberg in early May. Fassberg continued to serve as a training center and by 1943 the first Heinkel 177 heavy bomber (He 177) arrived.

The He 177 was a four-engined bomber with two engines mounted on each wing, not side by side, as customary, but in tandem. An odd arrangement to say the least, but dictated by the fact that this long-range heavy bomber was supposed to be able to fly as a dive-bomber as well. The He 177 is probably the worst example of German aeronautical engineering. In the Luftwaffe the aircraft gained the moniker "Luftwaffe Feuerzeug"—in plain English, Luftwaffe cigarette lighter.

The Junkers 52, affectionately called "Tante Ju" by German soldiers, served as Hitler's personal plane and served in the Luftwaffe to the end of the war in a variety of roles. The Ju 52 pictured is on display at the Museum of the United States Air Force in Dayton, Ohio. Photo provided by the author.

The He 111 was the principal Battle of Britain bomber and served in varying capacities to the end of the war, mostly on the eastern front. One of its unique missions was launching V1 rockets from over the North Sea against London, with limited success. Photo courtesy of Frederick McIntosh.

Its propensity to spontaneously catch fire in flight was caused by a faulty engine exhaust system, which accumulated combustion residue that would catch fire if not thoroughly cleaned out after each flight. Colonel Harold Watson who led Operation Lusty, the jet aircraft recovery of Me 262 and Arado 234 aircraft in April 1945, was an intrepid flyer, but one aircraft he did not cherish flying was the Heinkel 177. More detail on the aircraft and its employment can be found

This He 177 Greif in American markings was captured in 1945 at Toulouse Blagnac airfield where it was undergoing maintenance, and was flown by Colonel Harold Watson to Paris Villacoublay. Ernst Udet, who shaped the evolving Luftwaffe, insisted that all bombers be able to dive bomb. Udet saw the error of his ways too late and committed suicide in 1941. The aircraft crashed on takeoff from Paris Orly airfield because of a blown tire. German aircraft tires were notoriously bad. All He 177s were scrapped and no surviving aircraft of the type exist. Photo courtesy of Frederick McIntosh.

in my book *Watson's Whizzers*, the story of Operation Lusty and Projects Overcast and Paperclip. When living in the Trauen refugee camp in 1947, on my way to school in Fassberg I had to walk through the forest parking areas for Ju 88 and He 177 aircraft. I often sat in the cockpits playing pilot. I liked the Ju 88 best; however, my legs were too short to reach the rudder pedals which frustrated me greatly. I did not see one He 111 at Fassberg, they were all destroyed and used as barriers in the planned defense of the air base when British troops approached the airfield in April 1945.

By 1944 Fassberg lay in the path of British bombers heading for Berlin and experienced a fair number of low-level strafing attacks from British night fighters. The air base was directed to briefly turn on its landing lights when German night fighters attempted to land. Of course the lights were also visible to cruising Mosquito fighters, and a number of the German aircraft were shot down on their final approaches. Me 262 jet fighters appeared at the base, but they only flew a limited number of missions because of lack of fuel and other issues. By mid-April 1945 British tanks attacked the airfield approaching from the village of Trauen, where a couple of years later I would find refuge after fleeing from the Russian occupation zone. On April 16, 1945, it was all over. Surprisingly, the town of Fassberg itself suffered very little war-related damage, and the airfield itself, harassed by Allied fighters, was not a target of a major bombing raid. Several Me 262 jet fighters were captured at Fassberg and flown by the RAF.

The last major combat operation flown by Kampfgeschwader 4, KG 4, based at Fassberg, and associated units was in June of 1944. The wing at the time was equipped with He 111, Ju 88 and He 177 aircraft and still functioned as a schoolhouse for bomber crews. The United States Strategic Air Forces (USSTAF) commanded by Lieutenant General Carl "Tooey" Spaatz, negotiated the use of a heavy bomber staging airfield in the Ukraine with their Russian counterparts. Known as Operation Frantic, the idea was for American 8th and 15th Air Force bombers, after bombing targets in the east of Germany, to continue onward and land at Poltava and two subsidiary airfields nearby at Mirgorod and Piryatin, then refuel and rearm and make an additional bomb run on their way back to their bases in England or Italy. What looks good in theory doesn't always work out in practice. The airfields were declared operationally ready in May 1944, and 8th and 15th Air Force made some practice runs with F-5 (P-38) Lightning reconnaissance aircraft. On June 2, 1944, 15th Air Force, under the command of General Ira C. Eaker, launched Frantic Joe, 130 B-17s, escorted by 69 P-51s, with destination Poltava. Since Poltava and Mirgorod lay furthest east, the P-51s would land at Piryatin because of fuel considerations. On June 6, on their return flight, those same aircraft bombed airfields in Rumania, validating the concept of shuttle bombing. While at Poltava and Mirgorod the air crews were received with open arms by the Ukrainians, especially by girls who were thrilled to meet American servicemen. A good time was had by all, something not overlooked by the Soviet Kommissars, who promptly reported their misgivings to Moscow, which eventually resulted in the shutdown of Operation Frantic.

Operation Frantic 2 was launched by the 8th Air Force on June 21, 1944, using 117 B-17s and 70 P-51s. They bombed a target southeast of Berlin on their way to Poltava. I remember the raid well, although not knowing at the time what I was witnessing. Our air-raid shelter in Sagan covered one-fourth of the area under our apartment building, a housing development built in the mid-1930s for officers and civil servants at the Kuepper Fliegerhorst in Sagan. Sagan airfield in time would be the site for Stalag Luft III, a POW camp for Allied officer flyers shot down over Germany, which at its peak held over ten thousand POWs. In March 1944, seventy-six POWs escaped through a tunnel, seventy-three were recaptured, and fifty were executed by the Gestapo on orders from Adolf Hitler. The escape inspired the Steve McQueen movie, *The Great Escape*. According to the air-raid warden, that part of our building designated as an air-raid shelter had steel plates in the ceiling to protect us from bombs. I didn't believe her. I wondered how they could have known in 1937, when the apartment houses in our development were built, that there would be air attacks. Maybe someone was already planning war in 1937? They were, only little boys like me didn't know that. Two shelter windows looking northwest toward the town of Sorau, which had been bombed earlier in the year, were covered with perforated steel screens. The screens were designed to prevent bomb debris from entering the shelter window. I pressed myself against one of the windows and tried to focus my vision through the holes in the screen. I saw the American planes passing over or near Sorau on their second raid. There was little smoke after the bombs dropped, and instead of turning north,

A formation of B-17Gs from the 381st Bombardment Group, 1st Air Division, 8th Air Force, England, on their way to a target in Germany. Photo courtesy of the 381st BG.

the bombers kept flying east. After the bombers had passed out of my vision, I noticed a single aircraft following the Americans, higher than the others, sort of chunky looking. I wondered about that airplane.

Years later, when I spoke to my father about this event, he told me that KG 4 had sent up a Heinkel 177 bomber to follow the Americans to their new bases in the east. The He 177 photographed the three bases. The Russians wouldn't let the P-51s at Piryatin take off to engage the enemy bomber. After the first shuttle raid, the Germans prepositioned He 111 and Ju 88 bombers from Fassberg, and other KGs, at Minsk, to be ready for the next raid. The night of June 22, about 75 Heinkel 111 and Junkers 88 bombers attacked Poltava and Piryatin for two hours. He 177 pathfinder aircraft preceded them, dropping flares so the bombers could see the B-17s down below. Then the He 111s dropped their bombs and the Ju 88s machine-gunned the area. The Luftwaffe destroyed or damaged 69 of the 117 B-17s that had landed at Poltava, as well as 15 P-51s and numerous Russian Yak fighters, along with several C-46/47 transports.

German aircrew of KG 4 at Fassberg being decorated with the EK 2, the Iron Cross second class, by their wing commander after the successful Poltava air raids. Photo courtesy of the Fassberg Airlift Museum.

Over 450,000 gallons of high octane aviation gasoline went up in flames, along with most of the stored bombs and ammunition for the B-17's defensive armament. The Russians fired 28,000 antiaircraft rounds assisted by searchlights, without bringing down a single German aircraft. Poltava was an unexpected and embarrassing fiasco for General Spaatz. Air defense was a prerogative the Russians had insisted on, and it was a total failure. Whatever survived these attacks flew back to England several days later. Operation Frantic ended that September. Surely a lesson for future Soviet/American amity. As for the German KG 4 air crews, they were of course exhilarated by their success. However, that was to be their last major effort. There was not enough fuel remaining in the Reich to launch any future raids of that scope.

My father Willie had joined the 100,000-man army on January 1, 1929. He was three months and days short of his twentieth birthday when he did so, according to an entry in his *Wehrpass*. In 1933 he switched over to the newly created Luftwaffe which operated under a cover name and whose members wore civilian clothes, not uniforms. That all changed in 1935 when the Luftwaffe came out in the open, the same year the draft, *Wehrpflicht*, was reinstituted and Germany felt no longer constrained by the provisions of the Versailles Treaty. As the war progressed, in 1940, Willie qualified as a paratrooper, his assignment was to accompany landing parties into England to help establish an air base German aircraft could fly into. Of course this never happened. As a weapons officer he dealt with aircraft armament and bombs and was assigned to Kampfgeschwader 2 in the West, flying Dornier 217 aircraft. The combat wing's losses were so heavy that years later, when I told him I was joining the US Air Force and wanted to be a pilot, he tried hard to dissuade me from following my dream. He then was stationed in Holland at Soesterberg airfield and Gilze-Rijen before being transferred to Wiener-Neustadt, which was heavily bombed by the 15th Air Force, killing many of his fellow officers as they were having lunch in the *Offizierskasino*. Willie's commander had insisted he take home-leave, because he hadn't had home-leave for a long time, and his absence from Wiener-Neustadt most likely saved his life. His final assignment was at Fassberg Air Base where he was to work with the Arado 234 jet reconnaissance bomber, which never arrived. So he was put to work commanding an antiaircraft battery located in a potato field on the approach to the main runway. The 3.7 centimeter guns were near the barracks I was to live in in 1947, and on my way to school I would pass by them every day, now inoperable, not knowing at the time that my father had commanded those guns in 1944–1945.

While at Fassberg Willie had managed to obtain a house for his family in the Red *Siedlung*, the upscale officers' housing area. My mother, not familiar with what was going on in the world and not interested in anything but her own private life, didn't even read his letters, much less reply to them. Willie took some risk in his letters,

A He 177 and its aircrew. All the He 177s I recall seeing at Fassberg Air Base to the best of my memory had camouflage paint. Photo courtesy of M. Frauenheim.

because personal mail was opened and read, and he had to be careful what he said and still let us know how serious the situation was. Hedy greatly regretted her selfish mistake when we were in Berlin and learned of the Dresden bombing in February 1945, in which much of the Sagan population died sitting in railcars in the large switching yards. The people had been evacuated soon after our flight to Berlin, only to die a fiery death in a city everyone believed would never be bombed, because of its cultural heritage.

Life goes on. The big question was, now that the war was over, what would happen to the town of Fassberg should the airfield close down? Its only reason for existence was to support the Fassberg airfield, and without it there would be no employment for anyone, and the town would die. The answer to that question would evolve in time, but at that moment, in April 1945, it was an unanswered question that just hung out there, something the town's citizens worried about.

The numerous He 177s and Ju 88s at Fassberg airfield were of no interest to the British occupiers in April 1945. RAF 616 squadron, which arrived at Fassberg on April 26, flying Gloster Meteors, flew an Fw 190D, long nose, Yellow 8, formerly assigned to Jagdgeschwader/JG 26. The Meteor pilots of 616 squadron also tried out

This Me 262, flown by Oberleutnant Fritz Mueller of JG 7, then operating out of an air base near Prague, surrendered his aircraft on May 8, 1945, at Lechfeld. The aircraft is shown soon after landing before its German markings were removed. It became part of Colonel Watson's Me 262 collection returned to the United States on a British aircraft carrier. The aircraft is on display at the National Air and Space Museum in Washington DC. Photo courtesy of Frederick McIntosh.

two Me 262As, Yellow 17 and Yellow 7, both formerly of JG 7. When the squadron moved to Luebeck, they took the Fw 190 and the two Me 262s with them. White 5, another Me 262 fighter, formerly also assigned to JG 7, surrendered at Fassberg, and after being transferred to the UK ended up in Canada, where it suffered the ultimate indignity of being burned by firefighters in one of their training exercises. Yellow 5 was offered to Colonel Watson to return to the United States. Watson had enough Me 262 single-seaters assembled at Lechfeld and turned down the offer. It eventually was shipped to South Africa where it was scrapped in 1953. Finally, Black X, an Me 262A of KG 51, after being rotated through various RAF bases in England, found its way to Australia where it is on display at the Canberra War Memorial.

According to Phil Butler, in his definitive book *War Prizes*, "Aircraft of first-line fighter units were generally identified by an individual code number painted in a color which identified the *Staffel* (squadron) to which the aircraft belonged." Such as Yellow 8 and Yellow 7, and so on. Several *Staffeln* comprised a *Gruppe* (Air Group), and three to five *Gruppen* would make up a *Geschwader*, or equivalent to an Army Air Forces wing.

3

The Winter of 1947

The sun had not shone for weeks, and for a time it never stopped raining. Our compound swam in a sea of mud. The constant rain revealed the true state of our aging barracks. The roofs were leaking, and we had nothing with which to fix the problem. . . . Spiritually I began to feel as if I was slowly drowning, sinking into the sea of ooze around me.

—**Wolfgang W. E. Samuel,** *German Boy*

A fair amount of senseless destruction was committed by the German military before the town and air base of Fassberg were occupied by British forces on April 16, 1945. Three days earlier, referred to as Black Friday by locals, several very large bombs were exploded at the air base with devastating effect on Fassberg and nearby villages. If during the war years very little damage was done to the town, and none to the surrounding villages, this senseless destructive act did severe damage to windows, roofs, and structures. For the civilian population it was *unbegreifbar*, impossible to understand, how German soldiers could wreak so much havoc in their own land. After all, unless you lived in a dream world, by this date everyone should have known the war was lost and would be over in weeks, if not days. The weeks that followed were typical experiences—cleaning up and repairing war-related damage, organizing to again function as a town and community. The RAF commander encouraged and cooperated with such efforts and in time the little town built for war again found its equilibrium.

In late June 1946, with nearly no advance notice, families living in the Red housing area were ordered to leave—and to leave all of their belongings behind. The British posted guards on the selected streets to keep people from smuggling their belongings out of their houses. This approach didn't work totally at night; using their imagination people managed to smuggle out personal items of real or sentimental value. But all in all it was a calamity that had not been expected. English families then slowly were quartered in the empty houses. By Christmas 1946, the British base commander thought he needed to do something to improve Anglo/German relations. He invited the Fassberg mayor to his office and explained to him that he wanted to present the children of Fassberg with some gifts—such as cakes, cookies, chocolates, and so on. So the children of Fassberg had a Christmas after all. Relations between occupiers and occupied improved significantly after that gesture of generosity. However, life remained hard. German money was worthless, the black market flourished, and people made the best out of a bad situation.

I was twelve years old in 1947 and had a hard time relating to all that had happened to me in the past two years. I had survived the bombings in Berlin, survived some of the last battles of an ugly war, and survived Russian occupation. I survived our flight in a winter storm across the zonal border to the British occupation zone, and now here I was, a refugee in my own country, living in a rundown camp. I tried not to dwell on the past and instead looked for things that gave me hope of a better future, yet at night the past often caught up with me in my nightmares. I was lucky; my father had enrolled me in the Fassberg school and I felt fortunate in the knowledge that I was getting a real education again. On my daily walk to and from school I learned to love the pine forest and the heath with its juniper

Houses in the Red *Siedlung* taken over by the British to house families of personnel stationed at RAF Fassberg had a sign at the gate like the one shown—Royal Air Force Married Quarters. The Red housing development was the upscale housing area, the lots were larger than in the other developments and fenced as shown, not the case in the Grey or White *Siedlung*. Photo provided by the author.

bushes. Some of the bushes had weird shapes, and in the dark they appeared to look like men. I would stop in my tracks to assure myself that a juniper bush really wasn't a stranger coming toward me. In every case it was just a bush tricking my mind into thinking it was a human form. I was almost always alone. Few people had any reason to follow the paths I walked, and no other children from the barracks went to school in Fassberg. Sometimes when I stood still and listened carefully, I would think I could hear the tranquil sound of absolute stillness. For that instant, only the forest, the heath, and I existed.

My path from the barracks to my school in Fassberg took me first along potato fields and then through the pine forest which extended all the way into town. In the middle of the potato field stood a battery of light antiaircraft guns, three guns in the same

I learned to love the Lueneburg Heath, a sight of great beauty in August when the heath is in bloom; the juniper bushes at times became scary apparitions when walking past them in the dark. Photo provided by the author.

gun pit. I didn't know at the time that these were the guns my father had commanded. A scant half a kilometer from our barracks the Luftwaffe graveyard began. Most of the planes sat on the perimeter of the forest facing runways little more than leveled ground. Most were Junkers Ju 88 twin-engined medium bombers and Heinkel He 177 heavy four-engined bombers. I enjoyed climbing into the cockpit of one particular Ju 88, sitting in the pilot's seat, holding the control column, and imagining myself flying, just flying. The thought of flying was inspiring, made me feel free, like it would be something I could control. On its side, this particular Ju 88, had a four-leaf clover.

Aside from the Ju 88s, there sat too many He 177s to count. Some had been vandalized. Me 109s also were scattered throughout the area. Some had been flown by the English, with the German markings painted over with English roundels. One section of the aircraft graveyard held miscellaneous planes, among them a Ju 87 Stuka. There were no German jets anywhere that I could see. They must have been taken to England or had been destroyed in the last days of the war. A Ju 88 night fighter sat on a runway out in the open. I always intended to go and inspect it, but never did. A German company had begun to cut up the planes, loading sections of wings and fuselages onto a freight car parked on a siding of the small Trauen railyard. Before I knew it, the Ju 88 night fighter was gone.

That summer Mutti got a job on the air base. She worked at the NAAFE, the Navy, Army, and Air Force Exchange, where British airmen and their families shopped. She was served lunch there and was able to bring home some food for me. She took the English truck in the morning to the air base and came home the same way. My principal, Herr Soffner, who was also our homeroom teacher, informed my class one day that it had been decided for my class to receive an extra year of schooling, because in 1945 many children had missed a considerable amount of instruction.

Then Mutti lost her job at the NAAFE. The English were leaving Fassberg for good this time, or so it seemed to me. I had watched their slow departure since early summer, and finally they moved out most of the remaining airmen, putting the airfield in sort of a caretaker status. In the Red *Siedlung*, fewer and fewer of the houses were occupied, but not returned to their former German occupants. I used to see Spitfires and Tempests in the early morning hours, or late afternoons. Now, no aircraft flew into or out of the air base anymore. Losing her NAAFI job meant that Mutti also lost access to extra food, and again we were forced to live off our rations, the yield from our garden, and whatever any of us could scrounge. At times I would see a certain look in my mom's eyes, when she didn't know I was watching, a look of too heavy a burden carried for too long. I wanted to put my arms around her and tell her how much I loved her and that she had done well, that none of it was her fault. I never did. I began to worry that my mother might despair and do something awful.

Nearly everyone in our compound had lost their jobs at the air base, just as Mutti had. The only remaining employers were the potato seed farm in Trauen and the English army base in Munster-Lager. They had few jobs available this time of year. In Fassberg the beautiful houses in the Red housing area stood empty. I thought how nice it would be if we could live in one of those houses. The fields were barren again and the cold wind blew in off the storm-whipped North Sea and rattled the windows of our aging barracks. Loss of work meant the loss of meals once provided at work. It meant the loss of opportunity to supplement meager diets from the scraps of food discarded by the English mess or given by English families to their grateful maids. Loss of work meant having nothing to trade on the black market. It was totally dispiriting. If the English didn't come back, what then? Would Fassberg die?

In late February 1948 it turned bitter cold. A vicious blizzard blew up off the North Sea. Oma Samuel cautioned me not to go to school. I didn't listen to her. How could she know that I had to go, that nothing could keep me from going to my school? Nothing. Fortified with a cup of hot cocoa, I stepped resolutely into the raging storm and began my four-kilometer walk to Fassberg. The wind blew the snow horizontally across the frozen fields. It felt like it was sucking every bit of warmth out of me. I wore a warm English army parka with a hood, which my father had given me, and I carried my schoolbooks in a worn English army ditty bag slung over my shoulder. The wind died down a bit once I entered the forest. A few of the old Luftwaffe bombers still stood hidden under the trees, looking like fearsome weapons of war covered in their mantles of snow. My feet froze in my plastic wood-soled shoes, and my thin socks provided no warmth. I staggered through the forest thinking of the hot stove that awaited me in my classroom, blanking out the painful cold working itself up my legs.

I crossed the railroad tracks leading into the air base. I hadn't seen a train on the tracks in weeks. I followed the air base fence past the now closed officers' mess and finally emerged from the forest at the main gate. I turned right, down the concrete road. Normally I cut through the Red housing area, but with the English families gone, the streets were blocked by snow drifts. When I arrived at my school, I saw no one. The door was locked. My classroom was empty. There was no fire in the stove. I wanted to cry. I was so exhausted and cold. My heart sank as I stood outside my empty school with my feet so cold I could no longer feel them. I started the long walk back. Much worse than coming, I was now walking directly into the wind. Then the wooden sole in one of my shoes split down the middle lengthwise. I tied my belt around my foot. By the time Oma opened the door for me, I had no feeling in my feet.

My feet seemed like clumps of ice which didn't belong to me. I couldn't speak because my facial muscles wouldn't respond. Oma undressed me. She poured hot water from the ever-present kettle on her stove into two bowls. She made me sit and put my head, which she covered with a towel, over one of the bowls. "Breathe the steam deeply into your lungs, my dear boy," she said. She put my feet into the second bowl. I cried with pain and tried to pull my feet out of the water. Oma insisted I keep my feet in the hot water and suffer the pain. "Would you want to lose your feet my child?" Later Opa Samuel rubbed my feet forcefully in his warm hands to get my blood circulating, and then Oma put me to bed in the back room. She covered me with blankets and coats, until they were nearly too heavy for me to bear. By evening I had a high fever. Sweat was drenching my body. Oma would not let me out from under the covers. She put hot poultices on my forehead and chest. In the middle of the night I awoke painfully cold, shivering. Then I began to feel hot again. As I lay sweating profusely, Oma seemed pleased. "The fever will soon break," she said. Oma was right. I fell into a deep sleep all day and the following night, with Oma by my side the entire time, Opa later told me.

The day I returned to school massive snow drifts remained as the legacy of the blizzard. My grandfather had repaired the broken sole in my shoe. The bright winter sun shone on the wintry landscape. It

I am standing between propeller blades from Ju 88 aircraft left behind by the wreckers. This was on my way to school in Fassberg, where the German bombers had been parked at the edge of the forest. Photo provided by the author.

was incredibly beautiful. Here and there I could see tracks in the snow made by rabbits and foxes, and the occasional cry of a hawk pierced the stillness of my world. When I returned to school, I said nothing about having come to Fassberg during the storm. I apologized to my teacher for missing class because of sickness. "Fine," he said, "the school was closed for several days anyway. You didn't miss anything."

The free breakfast of hot chocolate and peanuts was discontinued. I had enjoyed every cup of hot cocoa and every handful of peanuts I had received. March passed with its eternal grayness. Life returned in April. Maybe things would get better in 1948? After the gray and cold of this terrible winter, people abandoned the prison of their rooms and spent every minute they could outside in the rare and invigorating sunshine. Windows were opened and old bedding aired. There was no paint, but people scrubbed walls and floors with water and rags and felt better afterward, even though the gray pine boards looked no different from the way they had before. There were smiles on people's faces now and then, and the women emerged from their barracks warrens with their babies and young children and stood in groups gossiping, many with hands held over swollen bellies. People watching and gossiping became the activities of the idle again. There were many men among them, since the RAF base at Fassberg was still closed, and everyone who had worked there was still out of a job. When I wasn't in school, I cultivated our garden plot and planted seeds for a future harvest.

Mutti and dad had reconciled their bitter differences enough to go through with their divorce. Both of them took the train to Celle, the county seat, and they petitioned the court for a divorce. The court granted their divorce based on my father's admission of his transgressions with other women. After that they seemed to get along much better. With the arrival of April, the dark, dispiriting winter of 1947–1948, which had nearly cost me my life, came to an end. The warming rays of the sun raised my spirits. There were signs, too, that better times lay ahead. On Fassberg air base there was renewed activity. The English started hiring again.

4

And Then the Americans Came

Lieutenant Colonel Harold Hendler flew some rather unusual cargo. On June 23, 1948, three days before the formal start of the Berlin airlift, Hendler flew boxes of the new German currency into Berlin. "My second unusual cargo was dynamite. At the newly built Tegel airport in the French sector of Berlin, the landing approach was over a radio tower used by the Russians. The tower represented a major impediment to flight safety. I flew the dynamite into Berlin, and the French used it to blow up the tower. Marshal Sokolovsky is supposed to have asked his French counterpart, 'How could you do such a thing?' The French commander's reply, 'With dynamite.'"

—**Wolfgang W. E. Samuel,** *I Always Wanted to Fly*

As April progressed, rumors of the Russians closing roads and waterways to Berlin circulated through our barracks. Some said the Russians delayed trains with coal and food at the border checkpoints, not letting them pass until many days later. Slowly, fear again rose to the surface of our lives—fear of becoming part of the ever-expanding Soviet empire. It seemed that for us refugees the war just would not end. One evening I overheard some men in front of my barracks talk about the Russians. I listened intently. A man whose voice I didn't rec-

Newly arrived RAF Dakotas in early 1948 at RAF Fassberg flying supplies to their garrison in Berlin. The Berlin airlift was yet to be approved. Photo courtesy of the Fassberg Airlift Museum.

The tent city at the former Trauen rocket research center housed hundreds of men who would do the loading and unloading of Mack trucks and aircraft at Fassberg, backbreaking work for little more than the food, clothing, and housing they received for it. Photo courtesy of the Fassberg Airlift Museum.

ognize, a stranger, said to the others gathered by my window, "I know for sure that the Russians stopped an American military train, but the Amis wouldn't let them. Maybe there will be war again," I heard him whisper. I thought my heart would stop when I heard the word war.

The stranger, who seemed to know so much, continued to talk to his silent group of listeners. "The English are not strong enough to stand up to Ivan," he said in a firm voice. "Only the Americans can do that. You all know that, don't you?" Some of the men nodded their heads. "Maybe the Amis will just go home. They don't need us." He paused. "Why should they die for us, die for people who were their enemies only three years ago?" The stranger looked around the group of men. I looked too. They stood silently, with downcast heads, some smoking hand-rolled cigarettes. "Whatever the Amis do," the man continued, grinding his cigarette butt into the mud with the sole of his worn German army boot, "we have no place to run. You understand that, don't you?" The men whispered among themselves a little longer, as darkness descended. Then they left silently for the barracks rooms they called home.

But neither the Americans nor the English abandoned us. Instead, within the next two weeks, there was noticeable new activity at RAF Station Fassberg. This time, curiously enough, it was not fighter planes I saw flying in and out of the air base, as I had expected, but twin-engined Dakota transports. The British version of the American C-47. My fear of war subsided with the sight of the Dakotas. The English were hiring Germans again. My mother got a job.

Shortly after the arrival of the Dakotas, the former Trauen rocket research center, adjacent to RAF Fassberg, was turned into a German labor camp. Hundreds of German men arrived, riding in the back of large British army trucks. They wore English uniforms dyed dark brown, and on their heads they wore strange-looking berets, just like the English soldiers wore. With childish curiosity I watched as they pitched their four-man tents on the grounds of the Trauen Center. "What do they call you?" I asked one of the men who was busy with

Entrance to the Trauen/Fassberg GCLO camp, the former rocket research center. Photo courtesy of the Fassberg Airlift Museum.

three other shirtless men erecting their tent. He straightened up, wiped his forehead with the back of his hand, and putting his hands on his hips said, "They call us GCLO men, young man. That stands for German Civil Labor Organization." Then he laughed, "But that is just a fancy name for plain laborers, which we are. Now, why don't you run along and let us finish our work." He was a tall man, with brown hair and large brown eyes. He looked intelligent, like a professor I thought.

An older neighbor boy who had found work at the air base told me the GCLO men were former German soldiers who couldn't find work. "They unload trucks and trains, and load English aircraft with supplies for Berlin," he said. "They work for their clothing, housing, and one hot meal a day." Then, as an afterthought, he added, "But the food is good." I later learned that they also got paid one D-Mark for each hour of work. As many as five thousand GCLO men eventually were housed at the former Trauen rocket research center, first in tents, later in Quonset huts, according to *Erinnerungsstaette Luft-*

bruecke Berlin (Kruppik et al.), published by the technical school of the German air force at Fassberg. Says Gerhard Noack, a former GCLO man quoted in the publication, "We had the best cooks from all over Germany. There was no shortage of food supplies. For breakfast we had oatmeal with raisins, toast, butter, and jelly." Lunch and dinner was equally ample. In spite of the heavy labor of heaving bags of coal off trucks onto aircraft, Gerhard noted, that in six months he gained forty pounds.

In the days after their arrival, when they had time off, the GCLO workers could be seen walking aimlessly around the small village of Trauen. There was little for them to do there. Soon a stranger from Hamburg built a tavern across the street from our barracks compound. He named the tavern Rote Laterne, Red Lantern, a name more at home in the raucous sailor quarters of Hamburg-St. Pauli than in the staid landscape of the Lueneburg Heath. The red lantern was a well-known symbol of prostitution, promising girls and sex. At least that's what my friends and I heard people say. The building itself—constructed of concrete blocks—remained unfinished on the outside. It was an ugly eyesore, even standing next to our gray barracks.

With my mother working, the pressure on me to scavenge for food was reduced. With the reopening of the air base there was enough work for everyone again. Trucks resumed picking up barracks people in the morning and returning them in the evening, as they had done in the past. No longer were my walks to and from school quiet and tranquil moments for reflection and dreaming. Instead I heard the intermittent thunder of straining aircraft engines overhead, the sounds of trains, their heavy cast-iron wheels again putting a shine on the rusty rails, and the distant roar of heavy trucks.

In April and May the haunting call of the cuckoo sounded through the forest and across the heath. Larks rocketed into the sky from their carefully hidden nests adjacent to the potato fields. Daisies popped up at the side of the dirt road I was taking daily to and from school in Fassberg. Flocks of grayish-black heath sheep,

My mother, left, with friends at the entrance to the Rote Laterne, an ugly building which functioned as a regular *Gasthaus* during daylight hours. At night it turned into a brothel. Photo provided by the author.

Heideschnucken, with long shaggy coats grazed on succulent shoots of grass, on young heather, and on upstart pine trees. All this, so familiar to me, was now joined by the new sights and sounds from the air base.

I heard that some GCLO men had formed a chess club and that they met in the Rote Laterne once a week. I went over to watch them play. I liked the mental skills the game required and learned it quickly. My mom was a chess player and played chess with Russian officers when they occupied our area back in 1945. She had used a small miniature chess set we had inherited from one of the German soldiers with whom we fled Strasburg. I asked the club president if I could join. To my surprise, he seemed excited to have a young boy join his club of old men. Old to me anyway. He started me off playing practice games, learning standard opening moves and how to protect my king and queen. When he thought I was ready, he allowed me to enter their tournaments. I soon became the champion of our small chess club.

In addition to the arrival of spring and the return of the English to Fassberg, there occurred an event of even greater significance to us *Fluechtlinge*. The *Waehrungsreform* was an event of such magnitude that it profoundly changed the lives of everyone. With this currency reform I decided that the war was finally over for me. The shooting might have stopped in May 1945, but I had never really felt that the war had ended. Our suffering had continued unabated for the next three years. In many respects it was worse after the shooting and the bombing stopped. The dying continued, only the victims now were mostly women and children, and the causes of death were different from before, not bombs and bullets, but hunger and disease, exploitation and abuse, wholesale rape of young and old by force or circumstance. I watched my friends die of hunger, cholera, and typhus, and all I could do was try to forget their faces and their pitiful whimpers as they begged God to keep them alive. I never quite knew what exactly would bring the war to an end for me. Now that it happened I knew that the new money was the event I had been waiting for. With the appearance of the new money, just one day before the arrival of summer, a war that began when I was four years old finally ended for me, at age thirteen.

On Sunday, June 20, my mother and I walked the four miles to Fassberg and stood in a long line to receive our share of the new Deutsche Mark, or D-Mark as it was quickly christened. Each of us, Mutti, Ingrid, and I, received forty Deutsche Mark. Suddenly, clothing, shoes, and food were available for sale without the need of a ration card. The three western zones of occupation instantly turned into a world of plenty—the world I believed I was going to find, yet didn't, when we first crossed the border fleeing the Russian zone in 1946. Goods that had long been hidden suddenly saw the light of day. Like mushrooms after a warm summer shower, peddlers on bicycles appeared, flooding our barracks compound with cheap goods. Many people spent their good, new money on bad, old things at grossly inflated prices. No one knew what something should cost. It had been a long time since people bought goods only with money, without ration cards or without giving something else in return. A state of persistent poverty and despair was now replaced by euphoria, and the timing could not have been better. With the confrontation between the Russians and the Western Allies over Berlin, there was plenty of work now at the Fassberg Air Base, work paid for with real money.

It wasn't only the purchasing power of the new money that changed our world of subsistence and deprivation. More so, it was what the new money represented for us—a new beginning, a fresh start in life. Maybe it would provide the means for a transformation from what we had become to what secretly we wanted to be. Maybe the new money would put a stop to the despised black market, the darkest aspect of our daily lives. It was, above all, a market that traded in sex. It forced women to view themselves as chattel, as goods, valued by another as being worth a few cigarettes, a pair of nylons, three or four candy bars, a can of coffee. A full can of coffee if lucky, and not many cigarettes at that, a pack or two. That was all. Two packs of cigarettes was the worth of a woman—it was the value of my mother, my friend's sister, my neighbor's daughter, the ex-Stuka pilot's wife. With the cigarettes or the can of coffee she received for allowing a man to possess her, the mother, sister, daughter, or wife would then try to obtain on the black market the food she needed for her children or her aged parents waiting for her in a home no more than a ruin—or an abandoned Wehrmacht barracks like ours. For me the black market at its worst was the memory of a small milk can filled with soup that my mother purchased with her body, the soup that kept my sister and me from starving to death in the brutal winter of 1945.

Although everyone at one time or another had to fall back on the black market to obtain something to keep functioning as a family, it was no frivolous choice. The family that did not count a young woman among its members was at a disadvantage in the day-to-day struggle for survival. The black market, the conditions of scarcity it thrived on, and our years of living in the rotting Wehrmacht barracks had stripped our lives to their bare essentials. Sex was so pervasive in our environment that it had become currency for us, the destitute. Personal humiliation was the daily norm, and most of us didn't even recognize for what it was anymore. The dirt of our lives was not only under our fingernails and on our unwashed bodies but had penetrated our souls. Barracks life, poverty, untold needs, and the usurious market that satisfied them ate away our self-respect. With the new money I hoped the black market would at least change its nature.

The warmth of the spring sun, the new money, a new job, and the general excitement surrounding the reopening of Fassberg Air Base also changed my mother. No longer did I see that haunted look of past violence and future fears in her eyes. Her face began to look younger, and she smiled and laughed again. As I looked closely at her over dinner one evening, I could barely discern the small scar on her neck made by a Russian bullet three years earlier. I knew there was a corresponding scar on the other side, it was nearly unnoticeable, but I knew it was there. I admired this brave woman—my mother, my hero, my friend. I was happy to see her smiling again.

The level of activity at RAF Station Fassberg had increased rapidly since April. I saw more and more English Dakotas flying into and out of the air base. And then one morning, on my way to school, I saw my first American plane. I stopped and gazed in incredulous amazement at this lone messenger of hope as it slowly rose into the misty sky. Spontaneously I thrust my hands into the air toward the vanishing plane and shouted, "*Hallo, Amerikaner!*" Tears of joy streamed down my face as I ran the rest of the way to school. I was excited all day long. I couldn't wait until my mother arrived home that afternoon to tell her the news—"The Americans are here." She understood, smiling at me as if we two shared a secret, and gently

My mother, sister Ingrid, and I, later in 1949 standing next to an American C-47 transport at Fassberg Air Base during an open house event. Photo provided by the author.

stroked my hair back with her hand the way she had done when we were under Russian rocket and artillery attack back in April 1945. I was terrified then and her gesture calmed me; I was excited now, and she knew how to calm me down.

All at once American soldiers appeared on the streets of Fassberg. Their presence provided me a sense of security that transcended all other aspects of our sudden and unexpected recovery. With the Americans around I felt safe. Being with us Germans, placing themselves on our side, trying to save our Berlin, meant to me that we Germans were not someday going to be part of the Russian empire. These soldiers, I thought, gave us Germans something very special, something war had lost for my country, and not even our new money could buy—friends. Good friends, I hoped, who would be there each tomorrow to help us if we needed help. I remembered what the stranger had said about the Americans only weeks ago outside my barracks—that only they could stand up to the Russians. And here they were. With the American presence I felt very safe. These American soldiers were different from other soldiers I had known.

Suddenly, instead of British soldiers or German security guards, there appeared young American MPs, military police, at the Fassberg Air Base gate. They were friendly and waved to me when I passed them on my way to and from school. Photo provided by the author.

They had come to help, not to take for themselves the little we had left. As a thirteen-year-old boy I just knew it was so.

There were so many wonderful things for a young boy to discover about the Americans. They were very different from soldiers I had known before—men with guns, whose faces were hard, and whose fingers were never far from the triggers of their guns. The American soldiers were not like that. They carried no guns, and they looked like people to whom life had been good and who didn't mind sharing their good fortune. That was a new concept for me to consider and get used to—being their friend, rather than a conquered enemy. The Americans, whose numbers grew by the day, flooded the small town of Fassberg with their presence. Soon a bar and restaurant opened its doors—Mom's Place. Mom's Place catered to Americans and was filled with young soldiers from early afternoon until midnight. The place was only a few houses from my school, and on my way home I could see the soldiers sitting outside enjoying the early summer sun, drinking German beer, laughing loudly, and smoking endless packs of cigarettes. If they were not smoking or drinking, they were chewing gum—just like the American soldiers I had met in 1945, always chewing gum. I never figured out why anyone needed to chew gum, but nearly all of them did, all the time. I loved them.

I watched the Americans closely. They wore what looked to me like tailor-made uniforms, of fine quality material, fitting for a Sunday suit, with shoes and socks of matching color. They wore their hats at a jaunty angle, matching their friendly dispositions, their carefree looks, and their relaxed and easy-going manners. They seemed to have lots of the new German money to spend. A rapid influx of merchants soon provided ample opportunity to spend it. The merchants set up portable tables along the *Horststrasse*, the concrete main highway that led into the air base, selling everything from fine Solingen knives with artfully carved stag handles to Bavarian beer steins, from Black Forest cuckoo clocks to fine jewelry from Idar-Oberstein. I walked past the many tables often and was surprised at the high quality of the things offered for sale. The soldiers, with their seemingly endless supply of money, kept the merchants smiling. Amongst them were money changers who operated out of the large pockets of their overcoats. As I watched them exchange D-Marks for American dollars, I discovered that an American dollar bought around twenty-four of the new German Marks. I had no idea how money was valued and by what measure an American dollar warranted twenty-four D-Marks. I had only received forty D-Marks when the new currency was issued, not even two dollars' worth. One thing about our new money—it mimicked the American dollar in size, not something we Germans liked. We liked what we could buy and do with the new money, but we didn't like its shape. And in future years when Germany was again an independent country one of the first things the politicians did was to change the shape of the American-designed currency, back to a larger traditional size and shape.

Women not from Fassberg appeared in town. They stood along the garden fences near the main gate trying to find American boyfriends. Many of them did, and suddenly there was a high demand for rooms in Fassberg. The supply was limited. For the right price, though, families were willing to double up and rent a room to an American and his girlfriend, who didn't mind paying the high prices they asked for. Some of my classmates had to give up their rooms. They smiled when they told me. Their families were suddenly prospering with the influx of so much money, money which bought real goods again.

My mother initially took a job in the English NAAFE, but she shifted to the American PX, or Post Exchange, when it opened. She was hired as a salesperson because she spoke good English, in contrast to me, I didn't speak a word of English. The PX was a large store which carried everything from expensive Swiss Omega watches to the much-prized nylon stockings and American cigarettes. Such items were not available on the German market and in great demand. Nylon stockings began to show up on the legs of Fassberg girls, a sure sign to us boys of who was going out with an American soldier. The Americans sold their Lucky Strike, Camel, Pall Mall, Old Gold, Chesterfield, and Philip Morris cigarettes right outside the main gate in plain sight of the military police. The cigarettes came in wax paper–wrapped cartons of ten packs, called a *Stange* by the traders. I knew when I saw an American airman exit the main gate carrying a brown paper bag under his arm, most likely he was carrying cigarettes, which he would sell before he had walked a hundred meters.

I was fascinated by the Americans, so different from any people I had ever met before. They drank wine and beer, and the few merchants in town quickly stocked up on a wide variety of German wines to meet the demand of their free-spending customers. Most of the Americans remained friendly, even when they drank too much, in contrast to the Russian officers I remembered. The Americans drank for different reasons, mostly for enjoyment. The Russians always drank to get drunk. There were English airmen at Fassberg too; after all it was an English air base. But the English kept to themselves. They were in no position to compete with the high-spending Americans. I heard women, smiling the whole time, endlessly talk to each other about the Americans, about what they did and didn't do, calling them "overpaid and oversexed."

Late one afternoon, our barracks Communist joined me on our front steps as I watched English Dakotas pass overhead. "Soon the capitalists will be gone," he said, smiling broadly. "Then the proletariat,"—a word I didn't understand—"will unite in East and West and we will live in peace as brothers and sisters, united in harmony, working toward a common goal. Ours will be a world of peace and plenty." The apartment of the barracks Communist was right behind ours, only a thin pine-board wall separated us. He had his bed right up against the wall. All winter long I had to listen to him groan on the other side. She never made a sound. Often it was late in the afternoon, and Vera would say to me, "Listen, there they go again," pointing to the wall. Mutti ignored the noises and acted as if she heard nothing. Day after day, if I was inside, and I was mostly inside during the winter, I listened to him having sex. I believed it should be private, but there was nothing private in the barracks. Now it was springtime, and his wife had a big belly again. I was appalled by his ignorant comment. Memories of life under the Communists flashed before my eyes—the spies, the beatings, the knock on the door at night, the prisons. Facing him, I stood up and shouted, "I have lived under your wonderful secret police. Why don't you take your family and move to the paradise in the East if you like it so much. No one is stopping you. I would rather die than live like that again." He jumped up as if stung by a hornet, looked at me with undisguised hatred, spit on the ground before me, and walked into his apartment. The barracks Communist never joined his comrades in the East to the best of my knowledge.

By late June, people in the barracks said that the Russians had stopped all traffic into Berlin. The city was totally isolated except for

Formally named the Regina Bar, the GIs quickly changed its name to something more to their liking—Mom's Place. It actually was the best and only place in Fassberg where you could go, relax, and have a good time. Photo provided by the author.

three air corridors from Hamburg in the north, one near Fassberg, and another corridor from Frankfurt to the south. I listened closely to the adults when they spoke of the city where I had lived in the early months of 1945. It was only a matter of time, some speculated, until Berlin was out of food. Then it would become part of the Russian zone of occupation. Maybe our Communist was right after all. I hoped not.

5

A Big Plane That Changed Everything

There wasn't one pilot who thought it wasn't going to work. Maybe there were some higher up in command who thought we weren't going to cut it, but the pilots thought what they were doing was going to succeed.

—**Lieutenant Joe Laufer,** from Wolfgang W. E. Samuel, *I Always Wanted to Fly*

By the middle of July ever more English Dakotas and American C-47s flew out of Fassberg. And then, in the beautiful month of August, almost from one day to the next, from one night to the next morning, a large American airplane appeared at the Fassberg Air Base. The new transport, very different from the Dakotas and the C-47s, had four engines instead of only two. And the aircraft did not sit on its tail like the others, but sat straight and level on its forward landing gear. Within a week the Dakotas had left Fassberg and the air base was filled with the large American four-engined C-54 Skymaster transports. From the day the C-54s arrived at Fassberg they began flying to Berlin, day and night, in good and bad weather. When the wind blew down the runway from the northwest, as it usually did, the C-54s turned over our desolate barracks compound every three minutes or so. At night I watched the exhaust flames from the four engines as the fully loaded aircraft strained to gain altitude over our compound, turning east to enter the northern corridor to Berlin, less than thirty kilometers from where I lived. I didn't know at the time that in future years, in wars yet to come, I would be flying with some of the men flying those C-54s, and that I would be gaining my own flying experience in some of the same aircraft now flying coal to Berlin.

My mother liked working for the Americans. Occasionally she came home accompanied by American officers. Pilots. They wore silver wings on their Ike jackets and silver bars on their shoulders. The Americans brought chocolates and cigarettes. They never stayed long. I could see in their eyes that they hadn't expected to find the poverty, squalor, and depressing grayness of a refugee camp next door to the clean and seemingly prospering town of Fassberg. It was a shock for them to see that people lived as we did. The sight of kids still mostly dressed in the oldest of clothing, the deteriorating barracks, the mud, the flies, and the always present smell of the common latrine made them want to return quickly to their clean, antiseptic quarters. If that didn't do it, once they saw the interior of our apartment—the woodstove with its pipe going through the ceiling, the water buckets, the worn furniture—they didn't want to stay around much longer. For whatever reason they had accompanied my mother home, they didn't seem to remember once they got there and quickly found an excuse to leave.

August always was the most beautiful month in the Lueneburg Heath. One sunny day followed another, and the heath bloomed in purple splendor. All the German aircraft had been cut up and removed, and I could enjoy the beauty of the land without the presence of the decaying tools of war. I had learned to love the land, in spite of the hard times my family had endured here. I abhorred the barracks, a compound of squalor and disease, but I loved the heath and Fassberg. They had become sustaining friends with their healing power when I needed them. When in August the heath was a

An American C-54 Skymaster transport being loaded by German GCLO workers at Fassberg Air Base. Photo courtesy of Robert Hamill.

blanket of purple stretching before my eyes to the horizon, I felt rewarded and rich for being able to share in the beauty of the land. Bees buzzed through the heath by the thousands, collecting honey for the long winter ahead. Shepherds emerged with their flocks of *Heideschnucken*, heath sheep, and the juniper bushes stood as silent guardians. I knew that one day I would leave the heath, but it would always remain a part of me. The American C-54 transports flew overhead, struggling to gain altitude in the warmth of the day. They too had become my friends, and like the heath, they belonged here.

When I walked to school in Fassberg and crossed the railroad tracks leading into the base, I now often encountered fully loaded coal trains arriving and empty trains leaving for the Ruhrgebiet to be filled again, to return and repeat the cycle. I had heard that the GCLO workers at first shoveled the bulk coal into army duffel bags, which they then loaded onto ten-ton trucks, the load carried by one of the new aircraft. Then the coal arrived already bagged. "One truckload fills an airplane," I was told over chess in the Rote Laterne by

A railroad crossing sign at the tracks I crossed on a daily basis; the sign was there since 1933 when the rail siding was run into what would become Fassberg Air Base. In April 1945 the sign attracted some unwelcome attention from passing British soldiers. Photo provided by the author.

The Fassberg Air Base locomotive. Photo courtesy of the Fassberg Airlift Museum.

my partner. "We load the airplanes by handing 20,000 pounds of coal from hand to hand until the sacks fill the interior of the plane. Each plane carries ten tons—20,000 English pounds. That's a lot of pounds, my boy." He paused to make his next move. "The twin-engined Dakotas, or C-47s, as the Americans call them, only carry two and one-half tons. They are too small and too slow, that's why the Amis don't use them anymore." My GCLO friend was all wound up that night, kept talking excitedly about the *grosse Luftbruecke*, the large bridge in the sky. "The Amis and the RAF fly into Berlin using the northern and southern air corridors, and the empty planes return through the central corridor. Our Fassberg planes only use the northern corridor. I bet you didn't know that?" My friend drew for me an imaginary grid in the air with his fingers, depicting Berlin and the three corridors radiating out from it to the western occupation zones. "And the Russians will shoot down any English and American plane that strays out of those narrow corridors," he added in a grave tone of voice. "The corridors are only twenty miles wide, and it is easy to stray left or right."

"That's pretty wide," I postured, trying to sound like I knew a little about what he was talking about. He immediately put me in my place.

"No, no," he said, wagging his finger at me. "That's not wide at all little boy." I felt myself blushing in embarrassment. But then he explained gently, "When you fly at 170 miles per hour it takes less than seven minutes flying time from one edge of the corridor to the other. At night and in bad weather it is easy for a pilot who is flying down the middle of the corridor to drift left or right. There are winds up there, you know, and they don't just blow from one direction and at a steady velocity. Once outside the corridor Ivan's fighters are waiting for them." He paused again, looked at me, and then with a sly grin he said, "You didn't know I was a Ju 88 pilot in the war, did you?" I didn't. He pushed the chess set aside, leaned forward on his elbows, looked straight at me, then whispered, "It makes me feel good to work with the Amis," and his eyes shone brightly when he spoke. In

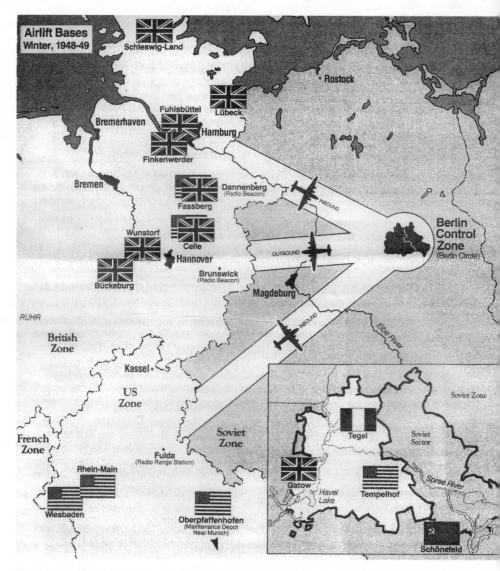

The Berlin airlift corridors were seldom interfered with by Russian fighters, although there were some rare occasions when that was the case. Photo courtesy of the Berlin Airlift Veterans Association.

a more normal voice he continued, "Let me tell you something else, my young friend. You know the Fassberg planes fly their coal into Gatow, don't you?" I nodded my head, but I really didn't know that. "It takes them an hour to fly to Berlin. They fly a straight-in approach

A Block-Time panel indicating that the first C-54 could start its take-off roll at sixteen minutes after the hour, and the last one had to be rolling at forty-nine minutes after the hour. If late by seconds, you would cool your heels until the next hour opened up. Photo courtesy of Joseph Laufer.

to Gatow, if they miss their approach they have to return to Fassberg—fully loaded. There is no second try. It's like an assembly line in an American automobile factory. A plane takes off right after one has landed and that cycle repeats itself hour after hour, day and night."

My chess friend wasn't totally correct in what he was telling me. The Fassberg C-54s took off in what was referred to as "Block-Times," one after the other, three minutes apart, for Gatow, in the British sector of Berlin; when Tegel was finished in the French sector, the Fassberg planes flew to Tegel and the Celle planes flew into Gatow. After their allotted time was up—maybe forty minutes—then aircraft from nearby Celle airfield took to the sky, also flying coal to Berlin. Fassberg and Celle were the two principal airports in the British zone of occupation which only flew coal. Others, such as Frankfurt and Wiesbaden, in the American zone, flew mostly food to Berlin into Tempelhof airport, in the American sector, and later, after it was built, into Tegel, in the French sector. Gatow, Tempelhof, and Tegel were the three Berlin airports into which most supplies were flown. Tegel, built from scratch by Berlin's famed *Truemmerfrauen*, rubble ladies, opened on November 5, 1948. The French did not participate flying supplies into Berlin. Their Ju 52 aircraft were too slow and would have interfered with the assembly-line fashion of the airlift. However, the British did fly supplies to Berlin out of Wunstorf, Finkenwerder, Fuhlsbuettel, Luebeck, and Schleswigland. While the American effort settled on flying the C-54 as the principal aircraft, the British used Yorks and Hastings, former bombers, as well as chartered commercial carriers.

"You are exaggerating," I said. "I can't believe it. They don't have that many airplanes." Another GCLO man who had listened to our conversation and joined our table said, "Werner is right. They fly, and they fly and they fly—like it is a war they are fighting. The Russians will not get Berlin, going against the Americans," pounding the table with his fist for emphasis, making my chess pieces jump, "I'll take any bet on that."

September, October, November passed. The days became shorter again; the nights longer and colder. In December it didn't get light until after eight in the morning and it was dark again by four in the afternoon. The rains came too, as they always had, interspersed with sleet or freezing rain. Our roof always leaked, no matter what we did trying to find and fix the leaks. I often ran out of containers to put under the leaks and just had to let the water drain through cracks in the floor. The big American transports continued to fly day and night, without interruption, regardless of weather. I heard the big planes turn over my barracks even when I knew the rain clouds were nearly touching the tips of the tallest trees in the surrounding forest. At night, lying in my old army cot, on my straw mattress, I thought about the American pilots: those brave men, whom I imagined sitting in their cramped cockpits holding on to their control columns, staring out into what must have seemed to them as blinding, impenetrable clouds. I didn't know how they did it. I wondered if they were ever afraid to fly. And I wondered how they found their way to Berlin in such ugly weather. And why they didn't crash.

On a clear December night one of the American C-54s turned over my barracks and then fell like a rock out of the sky. I didn't see it happen or hear it crash because I was inside, but I heard the commotion outside. Several men who lived in my barracks saw the plane fall to its death. "Not far from us," one of them said. Later I learned the pilot had banked too steeply and the coal had shifted in the turn. The two pilots and the flight engineer were killed. I went to the crash site after the Americans had removed most of the debris. The site was black from fuel which had seeped into the soft marshy ground. One engine lay half buried from the impact, useless now; another was barely sticking out of the ground I felt deep sorrow for the Americans who died here for us Germans. Only three years ago they fought against my country, bombed me when I lived in Berlin. Now they were dying to save Berlin. These Americans were strange people. I didn't really understand them, even though I had read about them, met them first in war and now in peace. I wondered, as only a child can wonder, what made the Americans do the things they did?

Opa Samuel had raised another pig, and he butchered it just before Christmas. Now we had plenty of ham, sausage, bacon, lard, and meat. The difference between this winter of 1948 and the one of 1947 was that everybody had work, new money, and hope for a better future. Christmas was a simple celebration, our first in three years with a very small Christmas tree.

In the spring of 1949, my mother came home from work at the American PX accompanied by an American sergeant. The sergeant wore the usual brown uniform with the Ike jacket and the large stripes on his sleeves. He was tall and lanky. I was immediately attracted to this American soldier, a feeling I never had about any of my mother's friends. I felt he was special, someone I would like to have as a friend. I watched him carefully. Standing in front of our barracks, he slowly and deliberately took a pack of Camel cigarettes out of his left breast pocket of his meticulously pressed Ike jacket, hit the new pack several times against the side of his left hand to firm-up the tobacco, and then opened the cellophane wrapper of the new pack by pulling a small, red cellophane string, which very neatly took off the top of the wrapper. Then he peeled away a section of the silvery paper wrapper, about the width of four cigarettes. Finally, he appeared to be ready to remove the first cigarette from the pack. He did this by hitting the pack against the side of his left hand. A cigarette popped out from the tightly packed package. Slowly he pulled the cigarette from the pack and put it between his lips, smiling at me as he noticed that I was watching him intently. Everything this man did was slow and deliberate, nothing hurried about him. I smiled back. Before lighting his cigarette he first replaced the pack in his left breast pocket and extracted an English Ronson lighter from his right pants pocket. Then, he lit his cigarette. He leaned his head back, as if to say, there is nothing better in life than a good cigarette—this cigarette. Finally, he took a long drag, blowing the smoke out of his mouth up into the air. I stood totally captivated by the American sergeant's performance. I had never seen anything quite like it before.

"My name is Leo Ferguson," he said, in a twangy, slow, American-English. "Call me Leo, please." He stretched out his right hand to shake mine. I noticed his fingers were long and slender, his nails clean and manicured. I didn't understand everything he said, and he could tell. "Leo," he said again, "I am Leo."

"*Ich bin* Wolfgang," I replied. He smiled a big smile; his teeth were regular and white, and his bright, brilliant blue eyes laughed at me. "W-O-L-F-G-A-N-G," he repeated very slowly, as if savoring the sound of the strange name. "That's a very fine name. I like that name." We both laughed. I felt instantly that he liked me as much as I liked him. I felt he didn't see any of the things others had seen in me, in our family, in our barracks—my worn out clothes, my sandals made

A Fassberg plane that didn't make it. Throughout the airlift the C-54 had a total of fifty-one major accidents, including crashes. Most were of a lesser nature, a truly remarkable achievement of flight safety considering the number of flights and the conditions they were flown under. Photo provided by the author.

from German airplane tires, the mud, the flies, the always present smell of the community latrine, the snot-nosed kids. And I hoped he wouldn't leave like others had. My mother joined us on the worn wooden steps in front of our barracks where Leo and I had sat down, side by side, close together.

Two little girls of three or four, with dirty faces and soiled dresses came scampering up, sticking their fingers into their mouths, unsure of themselves. They wore no panties and their thin, worn dresses barely covered their fat little bellies. They had been playing in the dirt in front of their barracks. There was nowhere else for them to play. The two innocent little girls stood in front of us, smiling, sucking on their dirty little fingers, looking at the American in his uniform. Leo reached into his jacket and pulled out a yellow pack of Juicy Fruit chewing gum, the same kind of gum an American soldier once had given me back in 1945 in another refugee camp. He took a stick of

Hedy and Leo, on the right, with friends at the Regina Bar, Mom's Place. After three years of sorrow, Hedy, my mom, could smile again. Photo provided by the author.

gum for each little girl and held them out to them. They took their fingers out of their mouths, giggled and hesitantly took the offered gift. "*Danke schoen*," they said in unison and ran off skipping and laughing to their barracks across the way to show off the gum they had received from the nice American soldier.

Leo, my mother, and I went inside, and Mutti served a simple dinner of potatoes and hamburgers in a brown gravy. Leo seemed to like it. After dinner they talked in English for a little while. I sat in a chair and looked at them, trying to understand the words. Then Leo got up to leave. He came over to me, smiling broadly he shook my hand and said, "*Auf Wiedersehen*."

"*Auf Wiedersehen*," I replied, jumping to my feet. I knew he would be back. After Leo had gone, Mutti told me that the sergeant had been coming to her PX counter for a number of days. "He stands around and acts like he is looking at merchandise, but really he is trying to work up enough courage to speak to me. Finally, he asked me if he could see me after work. I told him I lived four kilometers from the main gate. If he wished, and since it was a nice day, I told him he could walk me home." Mutti paused, then asked, "Do you like him?"

"Yes," I said quickly, "he seems like an honest and nice man. Yes, I like the American very much. His eyes are honest and warm and have no hate in them."

"I thought you would like him," Mutti responded with a smile on her face. "I like him too." Leo gave my mother some pieces of uniform for me to wear—one pair of precious uniform pants, a brown army shirt and sweater, and green undershirts and underpants, of which I had none to wear. I had not owned underwear for a long time and wore my shirt and my sole pair of pants over my bare body. It felt good to wear underwear once again. Of course, now that I owned underwear I had to wash it too, which I did every five days, or when it was dirty.

As the weather got warmer, I frequently rode out toward the air base on my mother's bicycle and met Leo halfway between Fassberg and our barracks, at the forest's edge, where the ugly four-engine Heinkel 177s used to sit. I waited for him, if he wasn't already there waiting for me smoking his Camel cigarette. We usually met around five in the afternoon. He always shook my hand first, then sat down again to light another cigarette in his usual deliberate manner. He would sit there for a while quietly, enjoying his cigarette. He seemed to me a man totally at peace with himself. I watched him fascinated, and respected the bonding silence between us, until he was ready to speak. Although he was a heavy smoker, I never wanted to smoke, and he never tried to get me to smoke.

When I felt it was alright to speak, I spoke to him in German— that's all I knew. When he spoke to me he spoke in English—that's all he knew. I listened attentively to what he said and at times I picked up a meaning because some words seemed to be similar to German words. Then I would nod my head and smile and laugh. Neither one of us fully understood what the other said, but we didn't need to understand everything. We both felt we communicated with each other, and with every day that passed I thought we became closer friends. I became drawn to Leo like a son to his father. I felt he cared. In his presence I began to feel whole, sheltered, and protected—feelings I had lost in the awful days of 1945 when my childish world had come crashing down. I had fewer nightmares now that Leo was around, and the faces of the dead I saw in my dreams had somehow softened, become less distinct; their eyes no longer reached for me.

One Saturday Leo asked me if I would accompany him to the air base, my mother translating. We left the barracks, riding our bicycles, taking the *Feldweg* across the potato fields into the forest. We followed the *Waldweg* along the railroad tracks leading into the air base. There were no guards or sentries to stop us. We rode across the base to one of the large aircraft hangars. Inside the hangar were C-47 aircraft no longer used in the ongoing Berlin airlift. Leo's room was at the top of the hangar, directly under the flat roof. We climbed an iron staircase leading to a balcony which ran along the roof line. Leo's room had four neatly made-up cots, their blankets tightly stretched. He took a coin from his pocket and bounced it off the blanket on his bed, "Regulations," he said, smiling at me. At the foot of each bed sat a green footlocker. Two metal cabinets stood against one wall. Each occupant shared one-half of a cabinet. I saw no locks anywhere.

Leo took off his jacket and undid his tie. He removed his shirt and indicated for me to do the same. Then he took two towels, two bars of soap, and a bottle of shampoo from his cabinet and motioned for me to follow him. I did, with some trepidation. We went to the showers. In the shower room Leo handed me a towel and a bar of soap and then pointed to one of the shower stalls. I think he said, "A shower will make you feel good," or something to that effect. Then he undressed and stepped into a shower stall. I watched him turn on the water. Steam soon rose from the concrete floor. As Leo began shampooing his hair he saw me still standing there. I didn't know what to do. At fourteen, I had never taken a shower. I hadn't even had a real

In the background, one of several large hangars at Fassberg Air Base with C-54 aircraft parked out front, during an awards ceremony. Airmen received an Air Medal for every fifty airlift missions flown. Photo courtesy of Robert Hamill.

bath in a real bathtub since 1945. Leo again pointed at a shower stall, for me to go in and do it. Reluctantly I took off the remainder of my clothes, but I could not get myself to take off the undershorts Leo had given me—so I entered the shower wearing my shorts.

Once I got the water temperature just right, I really enjoyed showering. It felt wonderful to have hot water bounce off my body— what a luxury! I took the bar of reddish soap and soaped myself all over, and then rinsed with more of the glorious hot water. Wow, what a treat. The soap had the word Lifebuoy imprinted on it and it smelled strongly of iodine. Not as good a smell as Palmolive soap. I thought about taking off my shorts, but I just did not get myself to do it. Leo was already out of the shower, dried, and dressed again when I finally turned off the wonderful hot water and got out. He said nothing about my shorts. I started to dry myself and then decided I had to take the big step and take off my wet underpants. I was sure Leo was laughing on the inside at my modesty and the predicament I had gotten myself into. But on the outside Leo remained calm, unnoticing, helpful. Once back in his room, without comment, he handed me a pair of dry shorts.

"Come on," he said, after I was finally dressed, "Let's go have a Coke." This time I understood clearly what he had said. After the shower episode, I liked Leo even more than before. For the first time in years I felt really clean. Not only my body, but also somehow inside myself where the grime of hopelessness and despair was slowly washing away. And I was especially grateful that he had not laughed at me for wearing my underpants in the shower. We rode our bikes from the hangar to the PX and parked them in an old, rusty bicycle stand. Near the entrance to the PX sat the crushed tail assembly of an Fw 190 fighter aircraft prominently displaying a swastika, a reminder of Fassberg's recent past. They had expanded the open area in front of the PX entrance by having a bulldozer clear and level the area of trees, bushes, and wartime debris, including an Fw 190 fighter which was in the way and crushed up against a rusty fence. No one seemed to pay attention to this reminder of a recent war. We entered the PX and came to a sign proclaiming SNACK BAR. I knew what the word *bar* meant, and thought the word *snack* must mean sandwich. A bar where you could buy sandwiches. That was an interesting twist on words, I thought. Who had ever heard of a sandwich bar? Only the Americans would come up with something like that. They were very unconventional folks I had decided by now, and I could expect anything from them.

Leo got each of us a Coca-Cola. The drink came in heavy glass bottles. He brought two glasses, straws, and ice. "*Setzen wir uns bitte,*" Leo said in good German. My mother must have been teaching him. We sat down and I enjoyed that wonderfully tasting Coca-Cola. I had never had a drink that tasted this good. I watched attentively the comings and goings of soldiers. Most wore work uniforms, baggy gray coveralls with big pockets, and caps on their heads with the bills turned up. It looked very funny to me to see these military men running around like that. Not very military at all. There wasn't any saluting going on either, and no heel clicking at all as German and English soldiers were prone to do. But then the heels of their boots

World War II had ended only three years before the Berlin airlift began, and here and there on the airfield and adjacent areas remnants of the recent past still abounded, such as this Fw 190 tail assembly and V2 sections on the Trauen rocket research center test area, shown in the next picture. Photo provided by the author.

were not made to click either. The Americans in their baggy work uniforms came and went to and from the PX on clumsy looking American bicycles with fat tires.

The Coke, as Leo called it, was an exquisite drink with a strange and wonderful flavor. I tasted coffee in it, or maybe caffeine. I let the Coke run over my tongue slowly so I could absorb its full flavor and to drag out the experience as long as possible. After our Coke Leo and I went to another part of the PX. I was overwhelmed by all the new smells, smells I had never experienced before. A strange mixture of pleasant odors emanated from boxes of candy bars—Hershey, O'Henry, and many more bars of different shapes. There was chewing gum of course, something the Americans didn't seem to be able to do without, and a large pot of steaming coffee, and donuts laid

out under a glass counter. Donuts, I surmised, were Berliners fried in fat with a hole in the middle rather than jelly. Leo just let me be. No hurry. He seemed to have a wonderful sense of knowing when another person needed time to absorb the new impressions rushing in on me. He lit another cigarette instead and got himself a cup of coffee and a Hershey bar for me. We returned to the barracks late that afternoon. It had been a wonderful day for me.

Leo frequently brought American friends along. On sunny weekend days they sat in front of our barracks talking. They would send me to the Rote Laterne where I would buy beer for them. Leo and his friends were generous with their beer and cigarettes, sharing with the German men who lived in the barracks and came over to talk to the Americans. As my reward for going to the Rote Laterne they gave me candy bars and chewing gum. When I had accumulated a fair amount, I didn't eat or chew it myself, I started to sell my goodies to the barracks children. Before I knew it kids from as far away as Trauen village came to buy my candy.

When I had saved up a fair amount of money, at dinner one evening, I wanted my mom's advice. My timing was terrible. Mutti had decided to tell a joke. She was a terrible joke teller. She laughed at her own jokes so hard that I rarely got the punch line. I tried several times to interrupt, but didn't get anywhere. "Here is one more story you have to hear, Wolfgang. Leo, you too. Then I stop," she gasped between laughs. "Wolfgang came to visit me unexpectedly in the hospital. You remember Wolfgang? November of '47?" She translated for Leo. "I was so happy to see you. I was depressed by my illness, for being confined to a hospital bed when I knew you didn't have enough to eat. Then, suddenly, there appeared Wolfgang like a ray of sunshine out of nowhere brightening my day. My dear son." She became serious, not laughing anymore.

"This is something I've wanted to tell you for a long time," she said looking at me. "That afternoon when I asked you to stay overnight, I thought there wouldn't be a problem finding a bed for you to sleep in. When I spoke to my nurse, she told me that the hospital was full. Every room was occupied, every bed was filled. Then the nurse had an idea. The room next to mine, the one you slept in, was the room where they put the dead for a night or two until they were picked up for burial. They had two corpses in there. The nurse put one corpse on a roll-away and put it in the operating room. There was no place anywhere else for the second corpse. They covered up the dead person with a sheet so you wouldn't see what it really was. The nurses made sure there was no light in the room by removing the light bulbs and pulling the window shades. They made up the bed from which they had taken the first corpse, and that's where you slept. I am so sorry. I couldn't tell you at the time. Are you angry with me?" How could I have been angry? It was my turn to laugh.

I remembered my question. "Can Leo buy me some boxes of candy and chewing gum with the money I saved from selling my gift candy?" Leo agreed to do so. And he lit a cigarette as he always did when something pleased him. I wanted to make enough money so I could afford to buy myself a pair of boots like the Americans wore. The Americans had boots made to order by German bootmakers. The boots came to just above the ankles and were easy to get into. I had dreamed for months of owning boots like that. The boots cost 147 D-Marks. Leo's friends kept giving me candy and gum for running their errands. Eventually I saved the money needed, and by May of 1949 I owned a pair of the coveted boots. They were my first real leather shoes since 1945, and I had bought them with my own money.

One little snag developed during this period when Leo was helping me make a little money so I could buy my dream boots. One evening he told me to meet him the following noon near the railroad tracks, where they entered the airfield. He would bring a parcel containing chocolates and gum and some other things. He rode his bicycle down the forest path alongside the tracks. It was a large bag, it turned out, which he had carried on a small carrier mounted on the back of his bicycle. Heavy. He waved goodbye and I went on my way. Soon I heard the noise of a car behind me. I turned around. It was a military police jeep with two American soldiers wearing a band around their left arms which read MP. They were nice and wanted to know how I got all those goodies I was carrying. One spoke some German and I tried to explain to him that my mother had received these things as payment for laundry she had done for an American. "Do you know his name?"

"Sergeant Leo Ferguson." So they loaded me into their jeep and off they drove to their headquarters, maybe two or three miles from where they had picked me up. They ushered me into an interrogation room where I soon met up with a German who was working for the Americans. The interrogator located Leo, and after Leo assured them that what I was carrying was for services rendered, they let me go. I was too timid to ask them to take me back to where they had picked me up. They probably would have done so. It was a very long walk for me to the barracks.

Spring recess ended. School began again. For the first time in years I had real clothing to wear. I was no longer uncomfortable,

The joint British/American police headquarters was located in the building that stood at what once was to be the main entrance to the airfield, but never served in that capacity. Photo provided by the author.

At age fourteen, in front of my barracks, wearing my treasured British army jacket and American army pants, which constituted my principal wardrobe at the time. Photo provided by the author.

ashamed at times, to be seen by my classmates or their parents. In school I was given a new name—Ami, because of the pieces of American uniform I wore. It was short for American. Calling me Ami was good-natured fun, and I took it as such. I wore my American uniform pants every day, my American army shirt and sweater, and my English army jacket if it was cold enough. I really wanted an American Ike jacket, but I didn't dare ask Leo for one. I could only dream.

A bookstore had been added to the shops across the street from the school. On my class breaks, when I wasn't playing schoolyard soccer, I went to the store to look at the new books and magazines. I was especially taken by a detective magazine about a private eye and his adventures in New York City. Every other week a new edition of the magazine appeared, and at fifty pfennig a copy even I could afford it. The detective's name was Kenney. Kenney lit a cigarette first thing in the morning, drank lots of black coffee, ate only nearly raw steaks, and always found his man somewhere in the canyons of Manhattan. I would buy the new edition the minute it appeared in the store, and read it overnight.

At our weekly chess club meeting, Werner, my GCLO chess partner, told me, "There are now three airfields in Berlin—Tempelhof, Gatow, and Tegel. Fassberg now flies to Tegel in the French sector of Berlin. "Do you know about Tegel?" He always did this thing, trying to impress me for some reason I thought. I didn't mind. "Know what about Tegel?" I replied. "I don't know anything about Berlin airfields."

"*Ja,*" Werner said expansively, "Tegel was built in only three months by the Berliners themselves. The runways were built from the rubble of bombed buildings. Isn't that amazing?" I agreed. "And then," he said, "a little while ago we opened a new airfield in Celle. They also fly coal from Celle, but to Gatow, not Tegel."

"Who flies food to Berlin if Fassberg and Celle only fly coal?" I asked. Werner of course had all the answers, as always. "*Ja,* the Americans have other bases in Germany, and they fly food from

The tower at Tegel, 1949. The newly opened airfield doubled West Berlin's capacity to receive coal flights from Celle and Fassberg. Photo courtesy of Joseph Laufer.

A Fassberg C-54 being refueled. Hard to imagine that a GI would have been able to drive a tanker truck filled with aviation gasoline off base all the way to Hannover to make a fast buck. But then, never underestimate American ingenuity. Photo courtesy of Leonard Sweet.

Wiesbaden and Frankfurt." Then he moved his knight and said in a conspiratorial whisper, "Checkmate." We both laughed.

At night, lying on my old army cot on my straw mattress, I thought about what Werner had told me. I thought about the Americans who were able to assemble a huge fleet of transports to supply Berlin from the air; just as they once assembled fleets of B-17 bombers to bomb Berlin when I lived there. I listened to the big four-engined transports turn over my barrack as I lay there thinking about them.

One weekend the Americans trucked all the German children from Fassberg and the surrounding villages to one of their clubs, a former *Gasthaus*, in the village of Mueden and fed them a huge dinner with Coca-Cola and cake for dessert. There also was a funny clown who made the children shriek and laugh. At fourteen, I was told I was too old to attend the party and could only watch through a window from the outside.

The black market was still with us, but its character had changed. Now goods were sold for money, not traded for other goods or sex. The black market was actually thriving more than ever with the introduction of the D-Mark and a need for nearly everything and anything. I listened to Leo one afternoon in front of our barracks as he was talking to a German man who had befriended him. He was saying that at Fassberg Air Base they had arrested a sergeant who wasn't just selling candy bars and cigarettes, something that was generally overlooked by the American military police. The sergeant worked in the motor pool and on two occasions had driven fully loaded tanker trucks to Hannover and sold both, the aviation fuel and the trucks, on the black market. We Germans could only marvel at the ingenuity and inventiveness of Americans. I wondered if they could manage to sell one of their airplanes as well without getting caught. At the moment the black market and the new German money were made for each other.

The American planes continued to fly their never-ending relays to and from Berlin. Another transport from Fassberg had crashed

Wreckage of another Fassberg C-54, which crashed in January 1949 on final approach killing the pilot. Photo provided by the author.

in January, Leo told me. This time on takeoff. He also mentioned rumors that the Russians were going to reopen the roads and rails to Berlin. The Americans just kept on flying. I could see it wasn't enough for the Americans to just beat the Russians and supply a whole city of two and a half million people with all their essential needs, so they made a game of it once the Berlin airlift had become routine for them. At an open house at Fassberg Air Base I saw a huge white banner draped across the front of one of the very large hangars; BEAT CELLE, it read, in large, black letters.

I asked Leo what it meant. He explained to me through my mom that Fassberg was competing with Celle to see who could fly the most coal to Berlin on a preselected day. I never found out who won the competition, but by June 26, 1949, the first official anniversary of the start of the Berlin airlift, the Russians reopened the rail lines and highways to Berlin. The Americans were gleeful to have beaten

Everyone showed up for the big parade and memorial ceremony to honor those killed during the Berlin airlift. A Fassberg hangar roof was the best venue for many. Photo courtesy of the author.

the Russians without firing a shot, a former ally who had turned against them. I was happy for the Americans too, but at the same time it saddened me, for I feared our American friends, and Leo most of all, would leave as soon as the airlift ended. After the Russians reopened the roads, rails, and waterways, the intervals between departing planes became increasingly longer. The drone of straining C-54 aircraft engines finally became infrequent during the day and ceased at night altogether.

At dinner one evening Leo mentioned that everyone was expecting orders to transfer. I knew once the *Luftbruecke*—the Americans called it Operation Vittles—was over, there was no reason for Fassberg to stay open. I didn't like to think about that. On July 29 there was a big parade at the airfield by American, British, and French troops in honor of those who had died in the airlift. My mother, Leo, and I went to watch. The next day Leo told Mutti that an announce-

An American troop contingent marching during the Fassberg memorial ceremony in honor of those who died during the airlift, July 29, 1949. Not until July 26, 1948, did President Harry Truman sign Executive Order 9981 abolishing discrimination on the basis of race, color, religion, or national origin. Desegregation was not immediate and the Kitzingen Training Center for Negroes was not discontinued until February 10, 1951. Yet our black airmen served our country with honor, in spite of it all. Photo courtesy of the Fassberg Airlift Museum.

French troops marching in the Fassberg Air Base memorial parade. The French had no airplanes to contribute to the airlift, however, they were supportive in other ways. Photo courtesy of the Fassberg Airlift Museum.

The C-54 that had the honor for the 60th Troop Carrier Wing of flying the last ten-ton load to Tegel airfield in Berlin on August 27, 1949. The inscription reads, "539,112 and THE LAST TON OF COAL FROM FASSBERG." The wing transferred to Wiesbaden on October 1, 1949, and Fassberg again became an all British Royal Air Force station. Photo courtesy of the Fassberg Airlift Museum.

My mother Hedy and sister Ingrid by a C-47 transport during the Berlin airlift memorial celebrations on July 29, 1949. Tail number 100737, I later learned, participated in the D-Day landings in 1944, and again in Operation Market Garden, as well as in the movie *A Bridge Too Far*. The aircraft is on display in a Danish aircraft museum at Stauning airport, Jutland, Denmark. Photo provided by the author.

ment had been made that the *Luftbruecke* would officially end on October 31, 1949. The next day the last C-54 flew from Celle to Berlin. Celle was closing.

A month later, on the evening of August 27, Leo told us that the last C-54 loaded with coal for Berlin had flown from Fassberg, and everyone had celebrated the occasion at a big party. Leo was a little tipsy when he arrived. "We'll be leaving very soon now," he said to Mutti. There was no need for her to interpret. I understood. On the last day of August my mother came home early with a wan smile on her face. "I've been laid off at the PX. That means I don't have a job anymore, Wolfgang," she lamented, "and I won't make any more money. Everything is closing now. It's all over. It's all happening so fast," she said in disbelief, and busied herself with some dishes. "Maybe Leo will know more when he comes tonight," she said. I said nothing. The good times were over for my mom, for me, for everyone—and I was deeply sorry to see the Americans leave. They had brought not only money to Fassberg, but they changed our very lifestyle with their openness and music and everything. They came from a different world, and I knew I would miss everything about them. The GCLO men at the Trauen rocket research center were also leaving. Soon they would all be gone, and there would be no more chess club in the Rote Laterne.

When I arrived home from school a week later my mother was waiting for me at our front door. She greeted me as I rode up on Leo's bicycle. "Hallo, Wolfgang. How are you? Come in quickly, I need to talk to you." I was indeed puzzled by her unusual behavior. She had never greeted me in such a manner before when I returned from school. I felt something important must be happening. But she didn't look worried. I leaned the bicycle against the gray barracks wall, locked it up, and went inside. She was sitting on our small couch behind the coffee table. "Come sit by me," she told me gently. I sat down close to her. She put her right arm around my shoulders and stroked some hair out of my face with her left hand, as she liked to

For the hard working GCLO men of Trauen, who had loaded by hand every sack of coal onto trucks and aircraft that made it to Berlin from Fassberg, there was no parade, they went the way they came, quietly, with hardly anyone noticing their departure. Photo courtesy of the Fassberg Airlift Museum.

do at times. "You are getting so tall, Wolfgang. Where has the time gone? I was so worried about putting food on the table, I may have missed something as you grew into a young man. You are fourteen now? Yes, of course, you are fourteen already, my dear boy." I wondered where she was heading with this strange conversation which made me feel rather uncomfortable.

She removed her arm from around my shoulders and moved away a little to face me. "Wolfgang, next week Leo is being transferred to another American air base in Bavaria. He is going to Fuerstenfeldbruck near Muenchen." There was a lengthy silence. She looking down, away from me. "Leo has asked me to go with him. Do you mind? I won't go if you don't think I should," she added hurriedly. I knew she meant it. It all came so quickly. What went through my mind at that moment was that this brave woman, my mom, who had sacrificed so much for Ingrid and me—she deserved some happiness.

"No, Mutti, of course I don't mind you going with Leo."

"Will you be able to stay by yourself?" she asked, looking a little worried and embarrassed at the same time.

"Yes, Mutti, I am a big boy now, as you just told me a minute ago. I can live here alone until school ends next year. Then I have to enter some sort of apprenticeship, if I can find anyone to take me. If you are not back by that time, we'll have to give up these two rooms. But there is no reason to worry about that now. Next year is far away. Go to Bavaria with Leo, Mutti," I told her firmly, getting up from the couch so I could look out the window and not let her see the emotion in my face. She rose, put her arms around me again, and kissed me on both cheeks. "You are such a good boy, and I am so proud of you. I'll write, and I'll come to visit for sure. It'll just be for a little while." We both cried.

The following week, in the middle of a glorious September, Leo showed up with a surplus Army jeep with USA and ARMY painted in white letters on its sides. On the hood of the jeep was a large, white American star. Leo and another sergeant had bought the jeep from the army to drive south to Bavaria. Leo drove, and his friend sat next to him. My mother and another woman sat in back of the jeep. Their things were packed in bags and boxes, stuffed all over the small vehicle. The little car looked hilarious, with its four occupants and every bit of space filled with gasoline cans, bags, and boxes. They were having a good time; that was obvious. My mom looked beautiful

How four people with all of their possessions fit into this little Jeep is beyond me, but they did it, and made it all the way to Fuerstenfeldbruck. The autobahns were empty in those days. Hedy in the middle, Leo's friend with his girlfriend at her side. Leo took the picture. Photo provided by the author.

in her happiness. The four of them drove off laughing loudly, waving to me and my grandparents Samuel at my side.

I wished I could have gone with them. I envied them. No matter what might happen to them, they had found a way to escape my world. I felt lonely. They looked to me like people who had a future. As the jeep disappeared down the road toward the small Trauen train station, I was sure that at least for my mother the barracks were a thing of the past—they were out of her life forever. I was happy for her. But her leaving me left a void. I was truly alone now, or so I felt, for the first time in my life. My little sister Ingrid had chosen to stay with my father, who had married a war widow with two children our age. She had a *Wohnung*, an apartment, nicely furnished. I didn't blame my sister for making that choice. She too had managed to escape the barracks. Oma and Opa Samuel were still there for me—I wasn't alone.

On September 27, 1949, RAF Fassberg returned to caretaker status. Mom's Place and the *Rote Laterne* closed. The American soldiers and their money were things of the past. German guards controlled access to the air base again, just as they had before the Americans arrived. An English soldier sat in the guardhouse where an American MP once sat. It was as if the Americans had never been here.

So much had changed since the Americans had come to Fassberg more than a year before. Because of them I was no longer afraid of the future. I knew they were our friends, even if they had left Fassberg. I also knew that because of them there would be no war. As I stood looking at the air base's main gate a strange empty feeling overcame me. I felt lonely, maybe abandoned is a better word, holding onto the handlebars of Leo's bicycle. I looked down the empty main street, the *Horststrasse*, and up at the silent sky. I missed the Americans and their noisy C-54s. I missed being around those confident, generous, and carefree people: the soldiers of the Berlin airlift, the people who liked to play games—to win.

The United States Air Force became a separate service in September 1947. However, the transition from the brown and olive-green uniforms of the Army Air Forces to Air Force blue was going to take time. At this time, based on my experience, every airman who participated in the Berlin airlift wore Army uniforms. Only towards the end of 1949, just before Leo and Hedy left for Fuerstenfeldbruck, Leo acquired a new Air Force blue uniform, and he really looked good in it. In 1950, when I visited, he always wore his Air Force blues; others still wore their old Army uniforms. In 1955, when, as an airman, I was stationed with the 7th Bomb Wing at Carswell Air Force Base, in Fort Worth, Texas, many of the older sergeants still wore their Army uniforms to show us youngsters that they've been around for a while. Much equipment that bore Army Air Forces logos continued to do so until it was retired. Only the aircraft were quickly repainted and bore the United States Air Force logo on their sides. The period 1948 to 1949 was one of transition for the newly minted United States Air

An American staff sergeant with three German guards at the Fassberg airfield main gate, April 1949. The guard on the right is wearing the new uniform, the other two are still wearing the old Wehrmacht uniforms. Photo provided by the author.

Force; however, in no way did that affect its effectiveness in carrying out its missions, whatever they may have been at the time. The Berlin airlift operation is a prime example of this—names may change, but the work goes on.

6

Flying Coal to Berlin from Fassberg

By August, construction of the south runway at Tempelhof was well along, but it was already apparent to Airlift Task Force planners that with more C-54s on the way a third runway would be required. However, even with additional runways, Gatow and Tempelhof were too cramped to meet the projected demands of the airlift. By late July, USAFE survey teams had found a former Wehrmacht tank training area in the French sector of Berlin. Plans for Tegel received approval on August 5. Operations (at Tegel) began on November 5, three months after construction began.
—**Roger G. Miller,** *To Save a City*

My personal experience of the Berlin airlift was that of an outsider looking in. For the men who flew and maintained the planes from a strange part of Germany it was quite another experience. Like most pilots who flew the Berlin airlift, Joe Laufer received his training in World War II. He ended up ferrying aircraft from the United States to North Africa, England, and Italy—B-26s from the Martin plant in Omaha; B-24s from Willow Run in Michigan; Douglas A-26s and B-25s from plants throughout the United States to wherever they were needed. "I got out at the end of the war, but I joined the reserves at O'Hare Field, and in 1947 the War Department recalled me and sent me to armaments school at Lowry Field in Denver, Colorado," Joe Laufer recalled for me when I interviewed him. "After graduation I ended up at Pope Air Force Base, near Fayetteville, North Carolina. Pope was the pits. The 82nd Airborne co-located with us was a really wild bunch. I went to Personnel to get out of there. They put me on the overseas list. It was August 1948. Instead, they sent me to Great Falls, Montana, for six weeks of C-54 training. From there I flew a C-54 to Frankfurt. In Frankfurt I was put on a military train to Fassberg. I had no idea where I was when I got there.

"I arrived at Fassberg at midnight. After a couple of hours of standing around and waiting, someone came and called my name. I was assigned to the 48th Troop Carrier Squadron. I grabbed my bag and a weapons carrier took me to a barracks and a cold room. That night I was flying. It was two weeks before I saw the ground I was flying over because of the weather. I flew coal into Tegel. We shared Tegel with the Brits. Timing was always critical, so we were assigned Block Times. Fassberg planes would take off between 16 minutes after the hour to 49 minutes after the hour, at three-minute intervals. If you got to the end of the runway at 50 minutes after the hour, you could not take off. Then you waited 30 minutes until the next block opened up. It happened to me a couple of times. If you had a Block Time of 49, for instance, often you had to play beat the clock because of some problem. We'd jump in the plane, start the engines, and while we were taxiing, we would run through the engine checks, pressures, and temperatures. Normally we would do this while sitting at the end of the runway. We'd taxi at high speed and check all four engines, and after that we'd run the before-takeoff checklist, hoping that by the time we did this and we got to the end of the runway, say at 49, the tower would let us go. And if we weren't quick enough, they'd say, 'Hold position and wait.' Then we sat there cooling our heels.

"I had the usual maintenance problems. One time at Tegel on one of the engines the starter wouldn't work. They had a shoe-like

At Great Falls, Montana, the Air Force established its training center for Berlin airlift pilots. The training simulated flying the corridors to Berlin and familiarized pilots with both the C-54 aircraft and procedures. The one thing they could not simulate was the lousy European winter flying weather. Photo courtesy of Robert Hamill.

contraption that fit over the propeller blades and was attached to a rope. The rope was wrapped around the propeller hub; in turn it was tied to a jeep. When the jeep gave the rope a pull, you had to have the ignition on and be ready to hit the mixture controls. It worked on the first try. One incident scared the crap out of me one night. As we went down the runway I discovered that the more speed we gained, the more aileron I had to crank in. Finally I broke ground. I flew to Berlin with the wheel cranked all the way to one side. The landing was tricky. As we decreased speed, I had to gradually decrease aileron control. It turned out that we had two hundred gallons of gas in the right wing tank. It was supposed to be empty. We had nothing in the left. And we didn't know it. Often the fuel gauges didn't work properly in an airplane, and just as often we didn't write them up. If

RAF Burtonwood was a maintenance and disposal center since the 8th Air Force moved into the United Kingdom in 1942. At war's end brand new P-51s, never flown in combat, were dismembered here. During the airlift of 1948–1949 Burtonwood provided the major overhaul capability needed to keep the C-54s flying. A second maintenance center was located at Oberphaffenhofen in Bavaria. Photo courtesy of Joseph Laufer.

we did, it grounded the plane. We were reluctant to Red-X an airplane. The airlift had to go on. As a result, many airplanes were in poor condition at the two-hundred- hour point when we took them to Burtonwood for overhaul.

"Visibility was our major problem. One time the visibility was so poor I could not taxi to the unloading area. The plane behind me was sent back to Fassberg. There was a Russian airfield in the take-off zone at Tegel. At about four hundred feet you had to make a steep turn to avoid flying over the Russian field. On one flight I saw Yaks lined up on the field. Later they were gone. They had these Yaks dispersing on different airdromes. Only two or three times was I buzzed by Russians. I could see them coming in the distance making a head-on approach, and then they would break off. I was never

A picture taken by Joe Laufer as he wandered through Berlin in 1948. Not only Berlin was a city of ruins, but so was nearly every other major city in Germany. Miraculously, when I arrived in Wiesbaden in 1969, after a combat tour in Vietnam, it was difficult to find traces of war—that's how quickly West Germany rebuilt itself. It was another story in the East. Photo courtesy of Joseph Laufer.

really concerned about them. After take-off from Fassberg, it was our practice to check in over Dannenberg beacon with our time and altitude. I listened to the aircraft ahead of me to adjust my airspeed to maintain the three-minute interval between us. At the Berlin beacon, approach control would pick us up—Corkscrew and Zigzag. Corkscrew took us to near the field, and Zigzag took us in. Those radar guys were the best in the world. They could bring you in through the eye of a needle."

Over a period of eight months, Joe Laufer thinks he flew 150 missions, "maybe a few more. I didn't keep a log, nor did most of the pilots, to the best of my knowledge. We just did the job we were trained to do—fly airplanes. There wasn't one pilot who thought it wasn't going to work. Maybe there were some higher up in command

Lieutenant Joe Laufer at a Tegel snack truck, getting a quick cup of coffee and a hamburger. The menu on the side of the truck offers hot hamburgers, egg salad, hot ham and coffee. Hopefully it was hot coffee. Photo courtesy of Joseph Laufer.

who thought we weren't going to cut it, but the pilots thought what they were doing was going to succeed." In eight months of flying Joe had three days of leave. He spent the time walking around Berlin. The city was mostly in ruins. Block after block of crumbling walls and empty holes that once had been windows to a gentler world. "I never met any Berliners. I hardly ever saw any of them, except when they were unloading my plane, or the girls at the snack truck. I thought of them as ordinary people who needed our help, not as former enemies." At RAF Fassberg, Joe's home base, he experienced culture shock. "The German maids when they came to clean my room would open the windows, regardless of the temperature outside. They were the original fresh air fiends. I would be trying to get some sleep after a night of flying, and they would come in, throw the windows wide open, and go about their business as if I wasn't there. In time, I learned to sleep through it all."

Colonel Robert "Moe" S. Hamill flew B-24s in North Africa and Italy. When the war was over, he got out and opened a little fast-food restaurant in Santa Ana, California. "One day an Air Force major came into the restaurant and asked, 'How would you like to fly airplanes again? I can get you an airplane so you can go anywhere you want. I can check you out over here in Long Beach. All you have to do is sign up in the Reserves.' I signed up. I was bored. This was in 1948, I hadn't checked out yet when I got a letter: 'Welcome to the Air Force,' it read. 'We need you for the Berlin airlift.' That's how I got back in. I went to Montana for C-54 training. They checked us out, then they sent us over to Germany. I ended up in the 29th squadron at Fassberg. My first flight was on April 13, 1949, my last on August 24, 1949. I flew 205 missions in seventeen weeks. I flew more than what my records show. On Tunner's Easter Parade I flew five missions which are not recorded in my records, but I know I flew them. I flew whenever I could.

"Most of the flying was boring, with the exception of one mission. We landed at the French base of Tegel. We carried coal and the British carried fuel. We'd sit there waiting to take off and watched the Brits land. The fuel baffles weren't too good on the Brit airplanes. When they land the fuel went one way, and they bounced. Then the fuel went the other way, and they bounced again. Of course we were supposed to observe radio silence, but every Yank out there said, 'One, two, three.' The Brits called back, 'OK, Yanks, shut up.' Every once in a while they'd have an accident.

"One mission I remember well was when Tegel was closed because one of the British fuel tankers had crashed. They diverted us

A crashed British Lancaster fuel tanker at Tegel airfield. The British focus was flying miscellaneous freight to Berlin such as fuel oil and salt, among other essentials. Photo courtesy of Robert Hamill.

to Tempelhof. On this mission I flew through my first really big thunderstorm. I remember going from 2,000 to 8,000 feet and back down again. We put on the lights in the cockpit, and the copilot worked the throttles. All I could do was keep the airplane level. First it was solid black in the cockpit, then with the lightning around us it would turn brighter than daylight. By the time I got to my GCA run into Tempelhof, I probably had lost ten pounds. Well, we were coming out of the clouds on final approach. I had never been to Tempelhof before. We were breaking out of the overcast. I looked to my left and saw that I was right in between these apartment houses. The windows were lit up. I became really frightened, because I knew I was going to crash. I added power. I was trying to get the power off. I landed so fast, I recall yelling for the copilot to help me on the brakes—we didn't have reverse props in those days. I used up the entire runway. It was that approach in between those apartment houses that frightened me to death. That thunderstorm made me forget everything.

"Fassberg was a good base. We never missed a mission, and I never aborted. Everything I remember was, 'Mach schnell. Mach

A HOWGOZIT board showed how each base was doing: Wiesbaden 60 GP (GP = Group), Rhein Main 61 GP, Fassberg 313 GP, Celle 317 GP, Rhine Main 513 GP, British 46 GP. The airlift became a very competitive affair, one reason why it succeeded. Photo courtesy of Joseph Laufer.

schnell,' hurry up, hurry up. I would get out there with the German crews and help them unload the coal from their trucks. That's how I got my exercise. Then we'd go down to the wagon and get coffee and a donut. All I did was fly and sleep. Three days off, ten days flying. Some days off I flew for guys who wanted time off to play poker." The German GCLO load crews at Fassberg, and at the other airlift bases as well, were a key element of the eventual success of the airlift. Although load and unload times for a C-54 usually hovered around fifteen to twenty minutes or so, a competitive spirit soon became pervasive throughout the airlift, including the German load crews. On February 11, 1949, a load crew at Fassberg set the airlift record of loading 13,670 pounds of coal into a C-54 in five minutes and 28.5 seconds. Moe Hamill knew what a great effort this represented since he not only flew the C-54 but helped on many occasions load the aircraft.

But all was not work for the airlift flyers. The spring and summer of 1949 was beautiful. Off duty American airmen strolled through the streets of Fassberg, a town untouched by war, looking for something to do. They crowded the few bars, sitting outside on sunny days, drinking German beer, smoking, and whistling at German girls passing by. Master Sergeant Chester J. "Jim" Vaughn is probably representative of many of the young single men who served in Germany at the time. Jim was an Indiana boy, grew up in the depression years. "Those were tough times for us," Jim recalled. "I learned firsthand what sacrifice was all about, so when I arrived in Germany in 1948 I could empathize with the German people. As a twenty-one-year-old airman, I did the job I was required to do as an aircraft mechanic." Jim was stationed with Moe Hamill at RAF Fassberg: Moe flew the planes Jim fixed. According to Jim, "When I was not on the job, I took the time to explore the local sights, keeping on the lookout for beautiful German girls. I found one, a lovely young lady, Ursula, who lived in the town of Lueneburg. After a fast and furious courtship, we were married in the Fassberg base chapel on August 17, 1949, and then spent a short honeymoon on the island of Sylt off Schleswig-Holstein, in the North Sea. In late September 1949 I brought my new German bride to the United States."

Jim and Ursula's marriage must have been one of the very first airlift-related weddings, but many more airmen were to marry German girls in the weeks to follow, including my own mother. Other relationships between young men and young women were more casual. Easy girls, referred to by Fassbergers as Veronikas, drifted to American military bases by the hundreds. One German thought Fassberg at this time was comparable to what happened during the Thirty Years' War, a time that was morally unhinged. The problems associated with many of the girls were a headache for squadron commanders. The commander of the 29th Troop Carrier Squadron, Lieutenant Colonel Elmer E. McTaggart was faced with the age old problem of what to do about it. He finally wrote a letter to his men on June 30, 1949, appealing for them to mend their ways:

Subject: Letter of Commendation

To: All Officers and Airmen 29th Troop Carrier Squadron (313th Troop Carrier Group)

1. Again during the month of June, the 29th squadron proved it was the best unit on the station. As we did in May, we carried more coal to Berlin in the greatest number of flights. We had the greatest number of aircraft in commission and the least amount of turn-around maintenance.

2. As a matter of interest, let me enumerate what the 29th squadron was leading in for the month of June:

   a. Greatest number of flights to Berlin.
   b. Greatest amount of coal to Berlin.
   c. Largest number of aircraft in commission.
   d. Greatest number of discrepancy reports.
   e. Greatest number of VD cases.

3. There can be no doubt from the above that we are the workingest, fightingest,———, outfit on the field.

4. It is a real pleasure to commend each individual in the fighting 29th for his part in the record we have achieved. It is a wonderful outfit and I am proud to be a member of the team.

5. It is nice to deal in superlatives when speaking of our squadron. However, I wonder if it is possible to eliminate discrepancy reports and V.D. rate from our list?

6. Each one of you is certainly entitled to a "well done." Let's keep up the good work.

/s/

Elmer E. McTaggart

Lt Col, USAF

Commanding

I have no idea how successful Colonel McTaggart's appeal was to his men, but three months later the airlift ended, and the girls who used to hang around the gate to the airfield disappeared along with the airmen to whom they provided so much comfort, and at times accompanying misery.

Others, not looking for girls of the night or life-time attachments, spent many of their off duty hours in the Fassberg Officers' Club playing poker, the American card game of choice in those days. You'd better not be a novice at the game or you would have your wallet cleaned out in no time. I recall, years later, during the Cold War, when flying reconnaissance out of Yokota Air Base, near Tokyo, Japan, the poker game in the Stag Bar went on around the clock, twenty-four hours a day, without any interruption that I ever knew of, and I was there for three months. When I returned to Yokota a year later, the game was still running. The Officers' Club for off-duty flyers at Fassberg was the former German *Offizierskasino* on the base, and in addition, a much more luxurious arrangement was available which went by the name of Flynn's Inn—a nearby plush hunting lodge which had been

Flynn's Inn, a hunting lodge used by the Fassberg Officer's Club of the Berlin airlift, was enjoyed by many on their few moments of free time. Photo courtesy of Robert Hamill.

beschlagnamed, requisitioned, by the British and made available to the Americans who at this time were running things at Fassberg. The British presence at Fassberg at this time was relatively minor. The poker game at this fancy former hunting lodge, many times frequented by Hermann Goering during the war years, may not have been continuous as the ones I remember from my Air Force days in Japan, but according to Colonel Hamill, it was in session most of the time while he was there.

7

The Ramp Rats of Celle

> So I had only been on the job for six or seven months when there
> came that all-important telephone call from General Lucius B. Clay.
> . . . Could we haul some coal up to Berlin? "Sure. We can haul any-
> thing. How much coal do you want us to haul?" "All you can haul."
> —**General Curtis E. LeMay,** *Mission with LeMay*

The first thing that comes to mind when speaking of the Berlin airlift
are the planes and their pilots. In the final analysis, they made the
airlift happen. Thoughts then turn to the vast tonnages of food and
coal delivered to a starving and cold city of over two million, the
number of missions flown and the men who died doing so. Often
forgotten are the men who kept those airplanes flying—who sealed
leaking fuel tanks, busted their knuckles trying to change recalcitrant
spark plugs, swept snow off wings with push brooms, and changed
failed light bulbs on two-story-high vertical stabilizers. These men
worked twenty-four hours a day in rain, sunshine, and snow to keep
the airplanes flying, to make the Berlin airlift a success. Rarely did
anyone think to run hot coffee and donuts out to the men on the line.
Rarely did anyone ask if they were warm enough out on the open-air
engine docks. Rarely did anyone wonder how they could change an
engine in the rain and driving snow. But the sergeants and airmen

kept working—grousing yes, even fighting back on occasion. The men on the line, the "Ramp Rats" of Rhein-Main, Wiesbaden, Celle, and Fassberg never neglected to keep their planes flying.

Former German aircraft mechanics were extensively used as well to balance airmen shortages. The incentives for the German workers at the time were one free meal a day, free clothing, and a place to stay. Each airlift base was given a quota of sixty-five German mechanics per flying squadron. There were no jobs on the German economy to speak of, so there was no problem finding applicants. Initial security concerns proved unfounded, and by the time the airlift ended, German mechanics were performing every phase of maintenance on the C-54, and they worked well with their American counterparts.

In early August 1948 the Royal Air Force decided to consolidate its Dakotas at Luebeck airfield, withdrawing them from RAF Fassberg and other installations operating this twin-engine transport. On August 21, 1948, the United States Air Force formally took over RAF Fassberg and flew its first C-54 loaded with coal to Berlin Gatow. RAF Celle, just a short bicycle ride from Fassberg, was also slated to accommodate USAF C-54s; however, Celle needed a lot of work and didn't fly its first airlift mission until December 16, 1948.

Tom Etherson arrived at Wiesbaden Air Base in early October 1948, from Japan, and immediately started pulling fifty-hour hour inspections. Tom was a New York boy with a wry sense of humor. "The maintenance area was set up between the runway and the taxi strips," Tom recalled. "When it rained, which it did for a week, we got wet—the maintenance docks had no overhead shelters. So we worked in the rain and slopped around in the mud for about two weeks until the inspections were completed. Although the maintenance docks were waiting for us, there was no room in the barracks. My buddies and I found space in the attic of an old German barrack. It didn't matter much since we were tired at the end of our shift. The food made up for it. The chow was great. The fact that it was served by pretty German girls made it seem that much better."

In 1947 Tom Etherson was assigned to the 317th Airlift Group at Tachikawa airfield, near Tokyo, Japan. "Duty in Japan wasn't bad," Tom recalled with a smile on his face when I interviewed him. "I worked on the C-54 aircraft engine maintenance docks. We had two men per engine plus the people needed for the general maintenance inspections, about fifteen men total per aircraft. We worked an eight-hour day, five days a week. The aircraft and engines were run through the wash rack before being towed into the covered docks. We used the checklists of Pan American Airways. Our working conditions weren't bad. Living conditions weren't bad either. A Japanese house-boy took care of the barracks for a pack of cigarettes a week. He made my bed and ran a rag over my shoes. The chow was plenty good, and there was lots of it. The vegetables were grown on a hydro-ponic farm. Most of the meat came frozen from the States, and the milk was made from powder. Our recreational facilities were great. A round of golf cost a quarter, with a nickel tip for the caddie, who, by the way, was female. The train into Tokyo was free. Although we had firebombed the city during the war, there was little evidence of it in 1947. The Ginza was a shopper's heaven. One of the canteens had been an exclusive club before the war, the Bankers Club. Not far from the Bankers Club was a bathhouse. Little girls with short slips led us into a huge tub made of marble. Once they got you into that tub, any thought of what might be under that slip soon faded. The heat made my entire body go as limp as a wet noodle. After that, one of the sweet things would give me a cup of hot sake. That's all she wrote. It took two of the girls to get me out of the tub. I couldn't even stand up. What did they do then, but shower me with cold water. Right about that time the army MPs would show up and write us up for not wearing a tie—professional jealousy of course, because the air force wasn't required to wear a tie with summer uniforms, but the army was. After the MPs left, we'd get a couple of rickshaws and head for the railroad station to the base.

"I think I got the word that my outfit was going to Germany the end of September. The leisure life came to a screeching halt. One-hundred-hour inspections had to be pulled on thirteen airplanes. I started to put in long hours. No longer was I free to take it easy when my engine was done. I had to help in other areas that still needed work. I turned twenty-one and celebrated my birthday at the Enlisted Men's Club. The day came when we said goodbye to Nippon. Our first stop was Kwajalein atoll. Our next stop was Guam, North Field. There were no facilities on Guam, so we slept in the aircraft. The mosquitos buzzed around inside the C-54 sounding like the engines were running. Our next stop was Hickam Field, Hawaii. After we serviced the aircraft in the rain, we found the NCO Club. It must have shocked the waitress because all of us wanted fresh milk. Most of us hadn't tasted fresh milk in a year or two.

"We got our first glimpse of the land of the big PX as the sun was setting. The sun made the Golden Gate Bridge look red. We landed at Fairfield-Suisun (later renamed Travis Air Force Base). We had a briefing by the commanding officer of what not to do in the land of plenty. Our next stop was Kelly Field in Texas, where the airplanes were winterized. We had four days in San Antonio. Those living close were allowed to go home for a couple of days. I didn't go, because New York wasn't considered close.

"Next stop was Westover Field in Massachusetts. We were not allowed to go into town because our transfer from Japan to Germany was supposed to be a secret movement. The military police looked the other way when we walked out the gate. I was at a bar in Chicopee Falls when the radio announcer said the 317th Troop Carrier Group was passing through on the way from Japan to Germany to join the Berlin airlift. He went on to say that you could recognize the troops by the 5th Air Force patch they wore. So much for a secret movement. After Westover we went to Newfoundland, the Azores, and then to Wiesbaden, Germany.

"One morning we were replacing an oil cooler, a messy job, when a man walked up to us with no hat, no insignia on his flight jacket, and a stub of a cigar in his mouth. One of the NCOs said, 'Hey, you can't smoke here.' The stranger replied, 'Don't sweat it.' He questioned us on how we were doing and what we needed most to keep the airplanes flying. Everyone had his own wish list, but no one thought to tell him that we had no winter clothing. When the stranger left the line, the chief came out of his tent, where he kept his huge potbellied stove going all the time. He asked us if we had seen a general. We asked him what the general looked like. It turned out that the cigar smoker was General Curtis E. LeMay." At the beginning of the Berlin airlift in 1948 General LeMay was CinC USAFE, Commander in Chief, United States Air Forces Europe, then headquartered at Lindsey Air Station in Wiesbaden, where I would be assigned many years later in 1969 after a combat tour in Vietnam.

"A plane caught on fire in the nose dock one night. Since we didn't have the luxury of the wash racks we had in Japan, an airman tried to improvise by squirting gasoline on the engine to clean off some of the muck. The docks were equipped with explosion-proof lights, but unfortunately the explosion-proof light cover in this dock was cracked. Poof. The dock burned. The engine and the deicer boots close to the engine burned. When the fire was put out, the aircraft was towed to one side of the dock. The next night the plane was still sitting there. I was told by the guy who sat by the potbellied stove to get the navigation taillight off the burned aircraft. I was standing on the back of a weapons carrier when the expediter and aircraft scheduler drove up—an officer. He was the one who checked on the status of each aircraft. He called out, 'Hey you. Will that aircraft be ready for the next block?' Now, 'Hey you' is not the proper way to address anyone who had been out in the cold all night, especially when the questioner was sitting in a heated vehicle. I told him it sure would be.

"The expediter said, 'Say sir.'

"I said, 'Sir.'

"He called in the tail number and drove off, never giving me another look. I have a feeling that the expediter and the guy who set the engine on fire disappeared forever, because I never heard or saw either one of them again.

"That night we got our first snowstorm. In the morning everything looked grand. When we reported for work to the guy who sat by the potbellied stove, he sent one of his clerks out to tell us to sweep the snow off the wings. We got some rope, tied it around our waists, and with a man on each end to keep us from slipping off the wings, we swept off the snow. We were moving along fine and having fun dodging the snow that flew over the wings when we saw this fellow walking towards us. It was a navy chief. He looked like he had just stepped out of a recruiting poster—creased blue pants, leather flying jacket, scarf, visored cap. Next to him we looked like the Germans loading coal on the C-54s. He told us to clean the snow off his airplane. I told him we would as soon as we got finished with ours. In the meantime, he should get back into base operations and stay warm. When we finished our last aircraft, we went back to our maintenance dock and went to work. A little later a guy came running up, saying, 'Look at the navy.' Out on the wing was the well-dressed chief, trying to sweep the snow off his plane and trying to keep from slipping off the wing at the same time. There were two or three officers standing around mumbling and snarling that they were late for takeoff because the chief had not cleaned the snow off the wings.

"That evening, when we had buttoned up the engines and I was washing my hands in gasoline, I felt a sharp pain in the knuckle of my right hand. I noticed a tip of metal sticking out of it. With my dirty fingernails, I scratched it out. I didn't think anything about it, because my knuckles were scratched and scabby anyway. A few days later the most ugly sore I've ever seen appeared on my hand. The entire hand blew up like a balloon. I went in to see the guy who sat by the potbellied stove and told him I needed to see the medics. I showed him my hand. He said, 'You wise guys from New York will do anything to get out of work.' The medic looked at my hand and said, 'We have to show it to the doc.' The doctor said that the hand was infected from the lead in the gasoline. Lead could cause blood poisoning. He gave me a bottle of sulfa pills and told me to keep an eye on my arm. If a blue streak appeared, I was to get right back to him. I was restricted to light duty, not on the flight line. The first sergeant, the guy who sat by the potbellied stove, and I were not the best of friends, and when I told him I was restricted to light duty, he said, 'Go hit the sack and see me in the morning for duty.'

"That afternoon I tried to guess what sort of duty he would have me do, probably cleaning latrines. I couldn't do clerical work. Come morning, the first sergeant told me to get out of my filthy fatigues because I was getting grease all over his orderly room. I changed into a Class-A uniform. By then it was ten in the morning. I was told to go to the headquarters on a bike and pick up distribution and leave it with the mail-room corporal. After I dropped off the distribution, I took off for chow. Went to a Gasthaus where the night crew hung out and started to enjoy Wiesbaden. The hand healed up a little too quickly, but I kept the bandage on anyway.

"After a while, I saw myself back on the flight line. We were preparing to move the outfit to Celle. My job was to park and service aircraft when they returned from Berlin. Not a bad job. We left for Celle on December 22, 1948, a day I'll never forget. We were rousted out of bed about five in the morning, had chow, and loaded our possessions—one barracks bag for each man. Our tools and equipment had been loaded the night before. In fact, we loaded up anything that was not bolted to the floor. We had no idea what awaited us at the place we were heading for, which no one had ever heard of. Just before we could get noon chow they decided to load our aircraft. The flight to Celle was only to last about an hour. The plane was colder than a grave digger's ass in Alaska. The heaters required a spark plug to generate heat, but no one had ordered any. The one-hour flight lasted five hours. The copilot was TDY from Washington, DC, and must have needed the flight time to draw his flying pay. It was dark when we arrived in Celle. We had to unload the aircraft first before anything else so it could be loaded with coal for a round trip to Berlin. We got to our barracks about one in the morning. We had beds, but the mattresses were still in Wiesbaden. We slept the best we could on our heavy GI overcoats. About six in the morning I got up and made for the latrine. It was dark, and the barracks had no power. I found a commode by the light of a Zippo lighter. I was wearing one-piece fatigues, and when I dropped them I was darn near naked. When I sat down, I noticed this cold air, like standing outside in the wind. I sat down and then jumped near three feet into the air. The toilet seat was gone. I sat there in the wind on the cold porcelain seat. The windows in the latrine were broken. I cursed the damn Krauts.

"On the way back to my bunk, I ran into a couple of airmen. We hadn't eaten for twenty-four hours. When we got into the chow line, we discovered why the British were so thin. We had a cold piece of fish and a slice of burnt toast. That was it. No seconds. The Brits said it was because of the rationing. We learned that the Brits separated the messing by ranks. The privates, PFCs, lance corporals, and corporals ate in the cellar. The sergeants, staff sergeants, and some technical sergeants ate upstairs. Master sergeants and the Crown's sergeants ate in the NCO club. I was a corporal—the second time around. I wished I hadn't been a wise guy, or I would be a sergeant and wouldn't have to eat in the cellar. Our first job that day was cleaning the hangar floor. Someone, probably the same crowd that had broken the windows and stolen the toilet seats, had chopped open fifty-five-gallon oil drums and rolled them across the hangar floor. In the couple of years the hangar was closed, bird shit and feathers, dead mice, and bugs had settled in the oil, which then turned into tar. We took a break for chow. The noon meal, supper, and midnight chow were the same—mutton with some sort of heavy flour and water mixture on top, plus tea. Those meals never varied for all the time I was in Celle. On Christmas day noon, I was standing in the chow line when the little Brit in front of me turned around and said, 'We're in luck today, Yank.'

"'How's that?' I asked.

"He replied, 'It's Christmas. We get double rations.' For a moment I saw a picture of turkey with all the trimmings. The dream only lasted for a moment. As soon as I stepped inside, I knew what they were doubling up on, only this time most of the sheep still had their coats on.

"Instead of working on the engines, I was assigned to the airplane general crew—checking hydraulic leaks, cleaning coal dust off the control cables, and because I was a wise guy from New York City, the guy who sat next to the pot-bellied stove designated me as the number one man for fuel-tank repair. The C-54 was a wet wing airplane, meaning the wing itself was a gas tank. When a leak exceeded a number of drips per minute, we had to open up the wing and find the leak. Dropping a wing access plate was no easy task. I had to place a jack under the wings and take the studs off the access plates. Once the plate was removed, it had to be cleaned so it could be put back on. Also, before I could put the plate back, I had to prepare a mixture of two compounds called Stoner's Smudge. This required kneading these two compounds until they had the consistency of bread dough. The more I kneaded the blacker it got, and the mixture stuck to my hands like another skin. If I was still stationed in Japan, I could have gone to the hot baths, and maybe the stuff would have come off. But there was only cold water in Celle.

"Before I could put the goop inside the fuel tank, any residual fuel had to be removed with a garden hose, and someone, usually the German helpers, sucked on the hose to siphon it out. My man Rudi said, 'It will ruin my teeth.' I thought he could die from a mouth full of gas. But no ill effects were ever apparent in either of us. When we got to town, many of the girls didn't want to have anything to do with the guys with the black hands. A lot of German civilians came by our table at the Gasthaus and asked us what kind of secret

Quonset huts at RAF Celle provided housing for German workers used to load coal and maintain aircraft. The same type of housing was provided at Fassberg/Trauen GCLO camp. Photo courtesy of Fassberg Airlift Museum.

weapon we were working on. Then they walked away laughing. The Germans who were working with us were great mechanics as well as great friends. They used our American tools. One wrench used to install sparkplug leads was a real knuckle buster. It took the Germans to figure out how to work that thing so it wouldn't bust your hands. Every time I went to tighten a sparkplug, the front end of the wrench would slip. The Germans made their own. I kept one for years and guarded it like it was gold. Another reason I will never forget our German workers was that they shared their food with me. In the evenings they were served at a soup kitchen as part of their pay. One man would pick up the soup cans for the entire crew and get the soup. They gave me a can, and I drew rations with them. Certainly it was better food than the slop served by the Brits. The poor Brits couldn't help it—they had so little themselves. Overall I must say we got along pretty well with the Brits and our German helpers.

"Fassberg was up and running a couple of months by the time we got started. Someone at headquarters decided that Celle should haul more tonnage than Fassberg. 'Beat Fassberg' was the battle cry around headquarters and other warm places where the coat holders hung out. Work, work, and more work for us guys out in the cold places. There was an eleven o'clock curfew for those of us under the rank of staff sergeant. The Brit military police would come into the Gasthaus and say, 'We'll be back in ten minutes.' The damn Americans would come and round us up immediately. There was no one to complain to. We worked a minimum of fourteen hours a day, seven days a week. By the time we got to town and settled down for a tall beer, it was time to pack it in. I still wonder today what kind of people came up with those curfew ideas. Some clown who was a reservist came over from New York and said there were werewolf gangs of German teens who would attack GIs, and that's why we had the curfew. The only teenage kids we ever saw were nice, and we gave them cigarettes, candy bars, and chewing gum.

"I had fun tormenting the sergeant who never left the side of his hot stove. We worked the entire winter in nothing heavier than a field jacket and a sweater. It was a cold winter. About the time of the Easter Parade—Easter Sunday, April 16, 1949, 1,398 flights delivered 12,940 tons of coal and food to Berlin, a one-day record—we were issued fleece-lined leather coats and jackets. A lot of German girls were walking around in them the next winter I understand. The guy who sat behind the pot-bellied stove and a couple of other clowns at headquarters came outside and patted each other on the back for the great job they had done.

"Originally we went over to Germany for thirty-days TDY from Japan. It wound up being sixty days, then ninety days. It didn't bother any of us single men. But many of the flight engineers had family back in Tachikawa. The morale got pretty bad. So they sent most of those guys home, and greasy mechanics like me who were supposed to know everything about the airplane were suddenly made flight engineers. While we sat up there between the pilot and the copilot, we had no idea what to look for. I wouldn't look out the window

British military police using an American jeep at Celle. They seemed to understand the needs of our troops a bit better than our own MPs. Photo provided by the author.

Budding C-54 flight engineers of RAF Celle. L to R: Sergeants Kedzie, Brooks, Stanton, Elliott, and Tom Etherson. Photo courtesy of Thomas Etherson.

because it was too scary. If the instruments were in the green, I just sat back and smiled. Come to find out that most of the new guys flying the airplanes were TDY from the States and hadn't had much time in the airplane either. What a crew we were. Things were different then. If a man said he could do the job, the retort from the boss was, 'Have at it.' I really think that all of us believed we could do anything."

Master Sergeant Martin Allin, who made his home in Tennessee after retirement, had previously served as a flight engineer, but he had not flown on the C-54. His experiences resembled Sergeant Etherson's. "The standard crew configuration for a C-54 was two pilots, a navigator, and a crew chief/flight engineer. During the airlift there was no need for navigators, so the crew was reduced to three. I arrived at Rhein-Main Air Base on November 30, 1948. I was a so-called crew chief/flight engineer in the States. I was debriefed in the base operations building at Rhein-Main. They asked if I wanted to fly. I said yes. I was immediately assigned to a flight, and a check engineer was to check me out. Get this: I had never flown before on a C-54 except once as a passenger. Away I went to Berlin. The checker showed me this and that on my way there and back. When we got near Rhein-Main coming back, he said, 'Sarge, you better hit the technical orders for the C-54 aircraft, 'cause I am going Stateside tomorrow.'

"'OK, who will take your place?' I asked.

"He laughed and said, 'You.' So I became a flight engineer on the C-54. I slept the first three nights on a first aid stretcher in the operations building. The weather was the worst in a century. A total fog bank across Germany. We flew anyway. We were covered with coal dust. The wings dripped aviation gas all the time. Our beards grew. We looked like rejects from hell. But what we did was outstanding and we saved the United States from World War III. It was the most important achievement of my twenty-five-year military career. Those 130 flights from Rhein-Main to Berlin made me proud to be a part of that great operation."

In the spring of 1989 long retired Master Sergeant Thomas Etherson and his wife, now residing in Las Vegas, Nevada, made a nostal-
gic visit to Celle, where forty years earlier he had served as aircraft
mechanic and flight engineer. "I got to talking to a girl who was showing us around the castle in Celle, which was all painted and beautiful. I told her what Celle looked like when I first arrived in 1948. The
castle was gray, and the beautiful park that now surrounds it wasn't
there. I told her about the broken windows and the missing toilet
seats in my barracks at the base. She laughed and said, 'You have to
have lunch with my husband.' The next day we met for lunch and I
met her husband Dieter. Dieter was ten years old in 1945. After the
Luftwaffe abandoned the base, he and his friends went out there and
removed the toilet seats and anything else they thought they could
trade on the black market. Because they were kids, they busted all the
windows. And anything they couldn't carry away, like the fifty-five-
gallon drums filled with fuel oil, they broke and spilled over the floors
of the hangars. There I'd been, back in '48, cursing the Germans, and
it was just a bunch of kids. Dieter and I had a good laugh."

The 317th Troop Carrier Group of the Berlin airlift days which
flew coal to Berlin out of Wiesbaden and Celle airfields in Germany,
didn't fade away, but is currently based at Dyess Air Force Base near
Abilene, Texas. Now known as the 317th Airlift Group it flies the lat-
est model of the C-130 transport, the C-130J-30. Not only that, but
my granddaughter Anna's first assignment right out of pilot training
in 2020 was to the 317th Airlift Group. She certainly has some big
shoes to fill, and I know she is up to it.

The men who maintained the C-54s, and all the other transports
used in the airlift, both American and British, gave the pilots the
means to bring the airlift to a successful conclusion. When credit is
given, the senior commanders come to mind from President Harry
Truman down to Major General William H. Tunner, then the pilots,
and rightfully so. But few ever give credit to those guys out on the
flight line, regardless of weather, making sure that when the pilots

arrive that airplane is ready to go. I recall from my own experience flying reconnaissance out of Eielson Air Force Base in Alaska the dedication of our maintainers. In the middle of the night I saw them on the slippery wings of our RB-47 aircraft in minus-forty-degree temperatures. They could only stay there for about ten minutes, then had to get back down to prevent severe frostbite. By morning the aircraft was ready. I experienced the same dedication during the Vietnam War flying out of Thailand. This time the temperatures were at the other extreme, yet those dedicated men always had our aircraft ready, never keeping time of the hours they spent doing so.

So I ran across this poem by a former B-17 pilot of the 483rd Bomb Group (H), flying with the 15th Air Force out of Italy. He wrote the poem in 1992, looking back on his life as an aviator. The poem captures how we aviators feel about our maintainers—and I would be remiss not to share it with you, for it perfectly fits the guys who kept the Berlin airlift C-54s flying:

The Silent Heroes

Through the history of world aviation
Many names have come to the fore,
Great deeds in the past in our memory will last
As they're joined by more and more.

When man first started his labor
In his quest to conquer the sky,
He was the designer, mechanic and pilot,
And he built a machine that would fly.

The pilot was everyone's hero
He was brave, he was bold, he was grand,
As he stood by his battered old airplane
With his goggles and helmet in hand.

To be sure, these pilots have earned it,
To fly you have to have guts,
And they blazed their names in the Hall of Fame
On wings with bailing wire struts.

But for each of these flying heroes,
There were thousands of little reknown,
And these were the men who worked on the planes
And kept their feet on the ground.

We all know the name of Lindbergh,
And we've read of his flight into fame
But think, if you can, of his maintenance man,
Can you remember his name?

And think of our wartime heroes,
McConnell, Jabarra and Ritchie.
Can you tell me the names of their crew chiefs?
A thousand to one you cannot.

Now pilots are highly trained people
And wings are not easily won,
But without the work of the maintenance man,
Our pilots would march with a gun.

So when you see mighty jet aircraft,
As they mark their way through the air,
The grease stained mechanic with wrench in hand,
is the person who put them there.

John Wolter

8

How It All Came About

> When, at a meeting in his office with Forrestal, Lovett, and Secretary of the Army Royall, the question was asked whether American forces would remain in Berlin, Truman said there was no need for discussion on that: "We stay in Berlin, period."
> —**David McCullough,** *Truman*

The Allied military victory in 1945 over Italy, Germany, and Japan seemed absolute and there didn't appear to be another major security threat on the horizon, according to the most optimistic looking for a peace dividend. Disarmament turned into a near frenzy as the Army, Army Air Forces, and the United States Navy and Marine Corps shed weapons and personnel as quickly as possible. With over twelve million men and women under arms as World War II came to an end, that force soon shrank to less than two million. The US Navy's fleet shrank from 6,768 ships to a mere 634. The Army Air Forces fared no better. In May 1945 the United States air forces in Europe, under the command of Lieutenant General Carl "Tooey" Spaatz, operated from 152 airfields and 226 lesser installations flying a grand total of 17,000 or so aircraft. By 1948, when the Soviets put pressure on the Western Allies, denying access to Berlin, USAFE was down to twelve permanent air bases and fifteen smaller installations with a total of

368 aircraft. Lieutenant General Curtis E. LeMay, CinC USAFE, had no modern jet fighters under his command. In his own words, "At a cursory glance it looked like USAFE would be stupid to get mixed up in anything bigger than a cat-fight at a pet show. We had one fighter group, and some transports, and some radar people, and that was about the story."

So when in January 1948 the Russians began to impede access to Berlin, there was no United States Army strong enough to take on the Russian tank armies. Disarmament had seen to that. What was left of the US Army in Germany was an occupation force of a constabulary nature, not a combat-ready army able to take on a well-armed and trained foe. Russian army personnel stopped a British military train that January en route to Hamburg from Berlin. The train was held for eleven hours, then allowed to proceed. This form of harassment became a recurring experience. That February the communists staged a coup in Czechoslovakia, adding that nation to their growing list of satellites, and most likely raising Soviet confidence that a stranglehold on Berlin would yield positive results as well. The stage was set to make a grab for Berlin, which seemed ready for the taking. The Western Allies didn't have to wait long for the next move.

On March 20 Marshall Vasily Sokolovsky and his staff walked out of the Allied Control Council meeting in Berlin, thus ending any opportunity for resolving differences over the negotiating table. On March 31, 1948, the Russians imposed a new set of traffic regulations for access to Berlin, abrogating earlier agreements. There were to be no freight shipments from Berlin to the West without Russian approval. And all military passengers and their baggage would be inspected. In effect, a partial blockade of the western sectors of Berlin had begun. Four American and British trains were stopped, then pushed back to their respective zones by Russian engines.

General Lucius D. Clay, the military governor for the American and British zones (Bizonia) and commander of US forces, was joined by General Sir Brian Robertson, his British counterpart, tak-

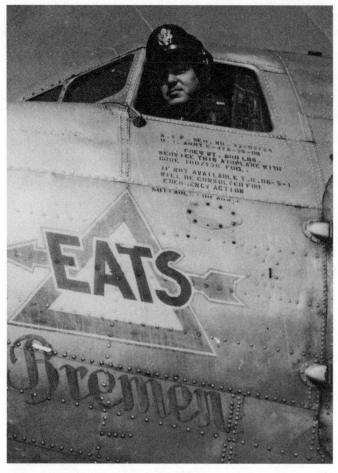

Lieutenant Sam Myers in the cockpit of his EATS C-47 at Bremen. EATS aircraft began the Baby Airlift on April 26, 1948, flying eighty tons of food into the city for the American garrison. Photo courtesy of Samuel Myers.

ing exception to the Russian provocations and on the following day, April 1, also known as April Fools' Day, began what would become known as the Baby Airlift. Clay and Robertson were not fooling, taking on the Russians head-on. The European Air Transport Service, EATS, composed primarily of aging C-47 transports began flying supplies from Wiesbaden and Frankfurt airfields to the American garrison in Berlin.

General Robertson followed suit and suddenly British Dakotas began flying supplies to their Berlin garrison from RAF Fassberg. Fassberg, the air base and little town built for war in the 1930s, suddenly found itself in a strategic location to provide airlift support. This time around, the Fassberg mission was not war, but just the opposite, to assure and maintain peace. Only days earlier the air base was practically at a standstill, and suddenly it came to life again, as I well remember as a thirteen-year-old boy living in the Trauen refugee camp at the end of the Fassberg landing strip. My mother and many of our camp residents suddenly found jobs again at the airfield. British families of flyers and maintenance personnel began arriving in numbers in Fassberg to support the nascent airlift effort, and of course were housed in the upscale Rote Siedlung, the Red housing development. Many housing units there were standing empty, because of the earlier draw-down, but shortly would be occupied again by British families.

Things were moving fast and furious in April on the political and military fronts. Army Secretary Kenneth Royall and General Omar Bradley, a World War II combat veteran whose accomplishments included the June 6, 1944, landings at Omaha Beach, suggested the evacuation of dependents from Berlin—truly a bad signal to send to the German population of Berlin, and a hint to the Russians that the pressure they had applied to Berlin was bearing fruit. In a teleconference on April 10 with General Clay, General Bradley expressed his belief that Berlin was untenable and that the United States should withdraw to minimize the loss of prestige. Clay viewed such proposals as alarmist and politically ruinous: "If we had started moving our dependents out we would never have had the people of Berlin stand firm." Clay responded to Bradley that the United States should stay in Berlin unless driven out by force. Bradley, whose daughter was married to an American Air Force officer stationed in Berlin, had him transferred back to the United States. General Bradley's son-in-law was not happy about his reassignment, but could do little about it.

The Baby Airlift was doing quite well and moving tonnages of food and supplies to their respective garrisons, including the French. That May Foreign Secretary Ernest Bevin, remembering Munich, declared in a speech to the House of Commons, "We are in Berlin as of right and it is our intention to stay there." This bold declaration was not lost on President Truman. On June 20 the three Western occupying powers announced currency reform for western Germany. Currency reform forced the Soviets' hand. On June 22 Marshall Sokolovsky announced that as of June 26 the new Soviet-issued Ostmark would be the only valid currency in Berlin. In response, the three Western allies promptly introduced the Deutsche Mark in the western sectors of Berlin. General Clay was convinced the Russians were bluffing all along to get the Western Allies to leave Berlin, and directed his deputy at EUCOM, Major General Clarence R. Huebner, to put together a regimental combat team, including armor, to proceed on the Autobahn from Helmstedt to Berlin. Once President Truman was informed of Clay's plan he promptly vetoed it, and usually supportive British friends also expressed their disenchantment with Clay's idea.

On June 16 the Soviet delegation withdrew from the Allied *Kommandatura* in Berlin, signaling that unpleasant things were about to happen, and they soon did. A week later, on June 24, the Russians cut the last rail links to Berlin, sealed off the roads, and stopped all barge traffic to and from the isolated city. In addition they cut off electricity to the western sectors of Berlin. The Russians weren't bluffing after all. It was about this time when Secretary Bevin got impatient and turned to his military commander, General Robertson, seeking a solution to the Berlin debacle. Air Commodore Reginald "Rex" Waite, responding to his commanders' request for possible solutions, presented a detailed plan on how to feed West Berlin, a population of two million plus, by air. Nothing like that had ever been done before. The scope of the proposal seemed enormous and not doable to many.

On June 25 Robertson acquainted Clay with the airlift proposal after first briefing Bevin. Clay thought he'd run the idea past his Air

Force commander and picked up the phone to call General LeMay in Wiesbaden. In *Mission with LeMay* the general recalled the conversation like this: "So, I had only been on the job for six or seven months when there came that all important telephone call from General Lucius B. Clay. . . . Could we haul some coal up to Berlin? Sure, we can haul anything. How much coal do you want us to haul?" Clay responded, "All you can haul." And the airlift was on. Clay recalled telling LeMay, "I want you to take every airplane you have and make it available for movement of coal and food for Berlin." Furthermore, according to Clay, "I never asked permission or approval to begin the airlift. I asked permission to go in on the ground with the combat team, because if we were stopped we would have to start shooting . . . but we didn't have to start fighting to get through in the air, so I never asked permission."

And so on June 26, the airlift began. The initial effort was feeble of course, but a beginning. American C-47 transports drawn from the European Air Transport Service in thirty-two flights delivered eighty tons of provisions from Wiesbaden and Frankfurt airports to Tempelhof airfield in Berlin. In Britain Secretary Bevin told the press, "His Majesty's government intends to stay in Berlin come what may." In a message to General Marshall, Bevin requested the immediate dispatch of American B-29 bombers to be based in Britain. And to finish it all off, on June 28 President Truman chimed in and ordered a full scale airlift to supply Berlin. However, there were still a fair number of high-level doubters who thought that this undertaking would never succeed. Undersecretary of State Robert A. Lovett again mentioned the option of withdrawal from Berlin to President Truman, who replied tersely, "We stay in Berlin, period." That July the Air Staff, of all people, was firmly convinced that the airlift was doomed to failure. Lovett continued to dismiss the airlift as unsatisfactory and a temporary expedient, and Secretary Royall predicted its demise that coming winter. Truman responded to his doubting staff by giving Clay all the C-54 aircraft he felt he needed—and Clay wanted every one of those transports regardless of where they might be located. Reluctantly, Air Force Chief of Staff General Hoyt S. Vandenberg surrendered his strategic reserve of C-54s to a jubilant Clay. Soon those coveted transports began arriving from Japan, Alaska, Hawaii, and the Canal Zone; every C-54 anywhere soon had orders to head for Germany.

At the start of the airlift there existed a lot of good will but little real knowledge of what it would take to supply a city of over two million people with its minimum daily needs. The first thing that had to be determined was exactly what was needed and how much. Then a determination could be made of what types and how many aircraft would be required to provide the minimum food and fuel to keep Berlin from going Communist. According to "A Special Study of 'Operation Vittles'" by *Aviation Operations Magazine*, the minimum food requirements for Berlin for one day were calculated in tons, not pounds:

46 tons flour and wheat	125 tons cereals
64 tons fats	109 tons meat and fish
180 tons dehydrated potatoes	85 tons sugar
11 tons coffee	19 tons powdered milk
5 tons whole milk for infants	3 tons fresh baking yeast
144 tons dehydrated vegetables	38 tons salt
10 tons cheese	

Strict rationing was implemented by the city of Berlin for various categories of people, ranging from 2,609 calories for heavy work, such as unloading the arriving aircraft, to 1,633 calories for six- to nine-year-olds. The nearly 1,500-ton daily requirement of food, when added together with coal and miscellaneous supplies, came to a total of 4,500 tons to be moved to Berlin every day. This led to the determination that 225 C-54 aircraft were needed to move the US portion of the daily tonnage. Initially, 102 EATS C-47s were used, flying from Wiesbaden Air Base and Rhein-Main Air Base, near Frankfurt. Eventually RAF Celle and Fassberg were added to the list of bases, strictly to fly coal to Berlin. A total of 201 Air Force C-54s and 24 Navy C-54s, drawn from squadrons throughout the world, were assembled at these four air bases by the end of December 1948. Having one type of aircraft, the 10-ton-carrying C-54 flying at 170 mph, vice the 2.5-ton-carrying C-47 flying at 150 mph, simplified the scheduling and control problems that a mix of aircraft created. To keep 225 aircraft flying, an additional 100 C-54s were in the maintenance pipeline at Burtonwood, England, and Oberphaffenhofen in Bavaria, for two-hundred-hour inspections or in the United States for one-thousand-hour inspections and overhaul. Nearly the entire inventory of C-54 transports was committed to the Berlin airlift—there was no strategic reserve held back.

The command and control arrangements, the fourth important leg for a successful airlift—the other three being aircraft, crews, and ground facilities—were soon in place. The British readily agreed to American leadership and on October 15, 1948, the Combined Airlift Task Force, headed by Major General William H. Tunner, began to operate from Wiesbaden. Lieutenant General LeMay, as USAFE commander, had brought in Brigadier General Joseph Smith once the Berlin airlift started on June 26, who immediately implemented the procedures to fly the Berlin air corridors. Before his departure from Germany to take over a floundering Strategic Air Command, LeMay arranged for Tunner to run the airlift operation. "Tunner was the transportation expert to end transportation experts. . . . It was rather like appointing John Ringling to get the circus on the road," LeMay wrote in *Mission with LeMay*. Tunner ran the famed China-Burma airlift in World War II, better known as flying the "Hump," as those dangerous flights over the Himalayas were referred to by air crews.

By mid-July B-29 bombers began to arrive at RAF Scampton in the United Kingdom, sending a clear message to the Russians. About the same time the RAF moved all of its Dakotas out of RAF Wunstorf and consolidated operations of this aircraft type at RAF Fassberg. Fassberg now was the home of about fifty Dakotas. While Americans had built new family housing areas near their military bases, including schools, churches, and shopping centers, the British relied totally on requisitioned housing for military families. The sudden influx of families who accompanied the movement of Dakotas from Wunstorf to Fassberg presented some problems. Of course the British families were settled in the upscale Red housing area of Fassberg. What to do with the German families who now were out on the street? An innovative German engineer and a man with contacts at the political level came up with the solution. Build not traditional brick houses, but instead use prefabricated parts and walls and what-have-you to put up houses quickly to satisfy an urgent need. The necessary money was found, and when I, as a thirteen-year-old, walked down the Poitzenerstrasse to my friend Wolfgang Luthmer's house, I could watch the houses go up very, very fast. In a way I understood that what was going on here was probably going to be the solution for Germany as a whole to find new ways to rebuild a land that was largely a field of rubble.

Once the political decisions were made, the military commanders organized the how, the where, the what, and the when until the Berlin airlift, Operation Vittles for the Americans, Plainfare for the British, became a routine operation. Generals Tunner and Smith developed efficient flight patterns, upgraded and expanded air bases as necessary, and all in all kept operations simple. For instance, it was determined that coal in sacks, early on in duffel bags, loaded by men, was the most efficient way of doing it, rather than using mechanical loaders. As a result hundreds of GCLO men housed in tents, later on in Quonset huts, at the former rocket research center in Trauen provided the necessary muscle. They operated as teams and when at their best could load ten tons of coal onto a C-54 aircraft in less than fifteen minutes. The planners determined that air bases in the British zone were closer to the Ruhr where the coal was

A squadron of B-29s from the 28th Bombardment Wing, Rapid City AFB, South Dakota, arriving on July 19, 1948, at RAF Scampton, near Lincoln, England. They were not nuclear capable, but the Russians didn't know that. Later arrivals had the Silverplate modification that made them nuclear capable. Photo courtesy of Joseph Gyulavics.

mined and as a result Fassberg and Celle flew coal, only coal. And Wiesbaden and Frankfurt flew coal and food supplies, while the British concentrated on delivering everything from fuel oil to salt. RAF Sunderland flying boats loaded with salt would land on the Havel River in Berlin to deliver this essential of life. In July Fassberg had just received an inflow of British Dakotas when in August the Dakotas were transferred again, this time to Luebeck, and American C-54s began to arrive to take their place. The USAF took over Fassberg on August 21, the day the first C-54 arrived and flew its first mission to Berlin loaded with coal the same day. By January of 1949 225 C-54 transports were flying in the airlift from four bases. This would be the peak strength of the American force, the slower C-47s had been withdrawn from airlift service and were used only in support roles.

On April 6, 1949, the US Army Support Command was established, assuming responsibility for all operations in direct support of the Airlift Task Force at the Rhein-Main and Wiesbaden air bases, and of course Fassberg and Celle as well. No one knew how long this operation was going to last, so a permanent, formal structure to support airlift operations was created. Then on April 16 and 17, 1949, General Tunner had his crews fly a maximum effort, the best you can do, which was referred to as the Easter Parade. From noon Saturday until noon Sunday 12,940 tons of coal was flown into Berlin on 1,398 flights. An incredible 80 percent of aircraft were in commission that day, with some groups reporting 100 percent—to get there you don't write up the little stuff, and that's what they did. Things were running like an American production line in Detroit, or better, making the naysayers eat their words. And the Russians began to get the message—Berlin wasn't going to be theirs after all; that became quite obvious. On May 12, 1949, they threw in the towel, as we like to say, and the blockade formally ended with the reopening of roads, rails, and waterways. Three days later, General Clay, who was greatly respected and admired by Germans, returned to the United States and retired from the US Army. General Clay not only saved Berlin with his vision and steadfastness but in the process of doing so successfully transitioned Germany from an occupied enemy country to one that one day would rejoin the free nations of the world. However, the airlift kept on flying to build up reserves just in case the Russians wanted to try it again. On July 29 Fassberg held a grand memorial ceremony for those killed in seventy major aircraft accidents, including thirty-one Americans, thirty-nine British, and thirteen Germans. British, French, and American troops participated in the parade that followed.

An official announcement was made on July 30 of the termination of the Berlin airlift. The official date when all airlift-related activities were to end was set for October 31. RAF Celle flew its last mission on July 31, and this active competitor of RAF Fassberg was no more. The only recently established US Army Airlift Support Command was disestablished on August 20. On September 18 Celle closed down and the last USAF elements departed. Obviously, RAF Fassberg's days were numbered as well—a scary scenario for a town

RAF Fassberg C-54s of the 60th Troop Carrier Wing awaiting redeployment after the airlift's end in September 1949. Photo provided by the author.

that was dependent on the air base for its life. Like Siamese twins, one could not live without the other. The future looked bleak. Fassberg did not have to wait long. Only days after Celle closed its doors, on September 27, RAF Fassberg was shut down as an airlift base. Its 60th Troop Carrier Wing was transferred to Wiesbaden Air Base effective October 1. End of story. The shutdowns happened as quickly as the airlift had started. To finish it all off: the last C-54 flight to Berlin was made on September 30, 1949, one month ahead of schedule.

The airlift was an incredible achievement of a combined operation between British, French, and American allies, which in a period of fifteen months in 277,569 flights of all kinds delivered 2,325,509 tons of food supplies and coal to the city of Berlin. General Lucius D. Clay, the revered military governor of the western zones of Germany, summed up the importance of the Berlin airlift: "If we had withdrawn from Berlin, which we would have had to do without the airlift, I don't think we could have stayed in Europe. I doubt if there would have been a Marshall Plan. I doubt if there would have been a NATO. How can you prove these things? I don't know. But I am convinced that if we had left Berlin, we would never have had the confidence of the West Germans, or of any of the Western Europeans. I think that if we had pulled out and the Russians had moved in, we would have lost confidence in ourselves. If they had succeeded in that, it would have started a whole chain of events. The airlift prevented them from doing that."

The C-47 and C-54 flyers who made the airlift a success were a hodgepodge of men with varied skills and experience levels. The only thing they had in common was that they were pilots or flight engineers. The lucky ones received C-54 training in Montana's blue-sky country; the others learned in the often -treacherous German skies. For at least six months of the year, Central European flying meant battling freezing rain, fog, violent thunderstorms, and frequent marginal visibility. Landings at Tempelhof airport with a maximum load onto short runways were more closely comparable to aircraft-carrier landings than to those on the up to 10,000 feet of concrete common at American air bases. The airlift was a "come as you are" operation, with no plans or procedures for handling the massive flow of diverse aircraft types into the restricted geography of West Berlin. In the early days, some people referred to the airlift as a cowboy operation, reflecting the chaos in the sky. The pilots had to learn to fly in narrow air corridors in all kinds of weather, making straight-in-one-try-only approaches into fog-shrouded fields. There were no sophisticated landing aids, just a world of ball and needle—compass, altimeter, attitude, and airspeed indicators. That there were not more accidents is a tribute to the adaptive skills of the American and British flyers. Skill or not, they could not have done the job without Ground Control Approach, GCA, radar, rudimentary radars by contemporary standards. The men who stared into flickering green tubes hour after hour, as well as the pilots who had to put their trust in the GCA operators' judgment, made GCA landings in zero visibility the system of the future.

The airplanes used in the Berlin airlift were severely punished in the "heavy load, frequent landing" environment. Maintenance focused on keeping the props turning. Fatigue combined with bore-

The draw-down at RAF Fassberg happened as quickly as the initial build-up. By early October 1949 all of the ten-ton trucks which brought the coal to the aircraft were gone. The last Americans leaving, the military police, shown here, had to use British trucks to take them and their baggage to an aircraft waiting to return them to the United States. Photo provided by the author.

dom became a real problem for many, as echoed in the stories I've presented. The Berlin airlift flyers conquered their unique challenges with skill and imagination. They did not disappoint the leadership that put its trust in them, nor the American or British people, nor the people of Berlin.

For flyers of the Berlin airlift, officer and enlisted, it was the kind of experience they would never forget. Amongst all of the boring missions flown in perfect weather conditions, there were always a few that made one wonder how he brought the plane down in one piece. For the flight engineers it was a never-ending task of keeping their particular aircraft, their tail number, flying. "Lucky" Lidard flew as a flight engineer out of both Celle and Fassberg. He also had a talent for poetry. Fifty years later, in 1998, he wrote the following lines recalling his days at Celle and Fassberg:

Airlift Memories

Lord! Yesterday was fifty years ago
Just where did the time. . . . just where did it go?
I didn't realize . . . I didn't know.
But then there's the mirror. The ravages show.

I remember. . . . really remember
That rainy . . . muddy, wet September,
The October fog and chill December
And . . . Oh Lordy! Do I remember?

There were some nights when I was terrified.
Many! Nights when I made my Berlin ride.
Exhausted! But that certain squadron pride
Pushed! . . . No, tugged me to nearly suicide.

No! Not of self-destruction . . . Not for me.
It was the bird . . . My bird . . . My tired beastie,
And few parts to fix my flying debris,
My plane . . . My comrade . . . My coal-streaked lady.

Day in . . . day out . . . and nights, we made the trip;
Dirty and tired . . . coal, coal, and straining ship;
Ice and fog . . . FEAR . . . Oil and fuel, drip, drip, drip,
And my final SCREECH . . . SCREECH on
Fassberg strip.

Lord! Yesterday was fifty years ago
And where did the time . . . just where did it go?
I didn't realize . . . I didn't know.
But then . . . there's the mirror. The ravages show.

Lucky Lidard was an intrepid flyer, and two years after his Berlin airlift experience he was flying RB-29s over North Korea and Communist China. There was the time when a flare bomb hung in the bomb bay of his RB-29—and it was Lucky who went out into the open bomb bay to chop the flare bomb down before it took all of them with it. He did it, just in time, watching the flare bomb ignite soon after it fell from the aircraft. Another memory for a man who earned his moniker 'Lucky' at Fassberg flying the Berlin airlift.

9

Then There Were No More Americans

30 September 1949. End of Operation VITTLES. Last C-54 left Rhein/Main for Berlin at 1845 hours, ending Airlift one month ahead of schedule due to sufficient food stockpiles in Berlin.
—*Berlin Airlift: A USAFE Summary*

I was alone in our two-bedroom apartment, not a real apartment, just two small rooms divided by a wall of flimsy pine boards. Mutti had gone with Leo to Fuerstenfeldbruck. My sister Ingrid had left with my father, who had remarried to a widow with two children Ingrid's and my age who had a normal apartment in Bad Oldesloe, a small town north of Hamburg. I had no idea how my father had met her. I felt abandoned, vulnerable and afraid. For the first time in my life, at age fourteen, I was totally alone, on my own. I knew I couldn't let such feelings persist. I still had my two grandparents, Oma and Opa Samuel. And there was Fassberg, my school. I quickly focused on these constants in my life and drew from them the strength I needed to be on my own for the first time in my life. I refused to feel sorry for myself; I'd been down that road before and it led nowhere.

I had a year of school remaining, then I would have to learn a trade or figure out something to make a life for myself. I knew I didn't want to be just a common laborer, but finding a place to learn a trade was something to worry about. My classmates with older brothers told me that it had taken them a long time to find anything, and then it wasn't necessarily a trade they wanted to learn. My biggest problem was that I had no idea what my talents were, or what I really wanted to be. Yes, I had that crazy dream, to be a flyer; to fly with the Americans. My impossible dream. I knew it would never happen, but I couldn't let go of it.

I did know that I wanted to read more, learn more about everything, and not just work with my hands. But that sounded more like school, and I knew that wasn't going to happen. I had missed all the gates—middle school, not to mention the *Gymnasium*, high school. I was a war child, even worse a *Fluechtling*, and no one really cared what happened to us. Something would come along, I consoled myself. Next year was still far off.

My Fassberg class, the extended eighth grade in our ninth year, was now the most senior class in school. We had become a close-knit group. I had made two good friends: Arnim Krueger, the only other refugee boy in my class who lived in an old German army barracks near the main gate, and Wolfgang Luthmer, whose home was in the *Graue Siedlung*, the gray housing development. I no longer felt as different from the others as I had in my first year in Fassberg. With the new money, plenty of jobs, and ample goods in stores, resentment against *Fluechtlinge* had waned. After school, the three of us often rode around on our bicycles, turning circles on the street in front of the stores or at the main gate to the air base.

Our principal teacher, Herr Soffner, organized a sports competition for our class in early September. We boys assembled near the soccer field to compete in the 50- and 100-meter run, broad jump, high jump, and 250-meter relay. The girls didn't compete; instead, they made up the certificates for the winners, and they watched us. We were to compete by year groups—1934 and 1935. During the first hour of the event we were given time to practice. I discovered that I could beat everyone in my 1935 year group in every event. I asked

Herr Soffner, also the school's principal, if I could compete in the 1934 year group. He agreed. While I knew I would be competing against one classmate in particular who was much taller than I, and who because of his longer legs could jump farther and run faster, still, I wanted it to be a true competition for me. If I stayed with my own year group, it wouldn't be. The tall fellow beat me in the high jump and in the two races; I came in second in both events. I also came in second in the overall standings for the 1934 year group. For me it was a real competition of my own making, and I liked that. I had striven mightily to beat my taller and longer-legged adversary, and I didn't mind losing to him. He had made me try much harder than I would have if I had stayed with my own year group. It was the competition that was important to me, not the outcome.

At night I missed having my mother around. As it got colder, I didn't light the stove. I piled more blankets on my bed to stay warm. I ate my meals at Oma and Opa's. Oma fussed over me just as she always had, when, as a little boy, I had visited her in their big house in Schlawe in Pomerania. Since I was with her nearly constantly now when I was not in school, she took full advantage of the opportunity to spoil her only grandson. She always managed to come up with a special egg dish or a cup of hot cocoa. I loved hugging my grandmother and giving her a kiss or two on the cheek, because she always acted like she didn't need that sort of thing. I knew better.

"Wolfgang, stop that," she would admonish me, laughing loudly. "You are such a foolish boy. You are getting my apron all ruffled, can't you see that?" And she would shuffle off laughing, straightening her apron. I loved to get my Oma all worked up. She was such a dear, and I loved her very, very much.

In December 1949 Mutti came on a short visit from Fuerstenfeld-bruck. She had written of her plans, and I met her at the train station. I was happy to see her again. She looked healthy and rested. That night she fixed dinner for us two, and it was almost like old times, but not really. I knew she would leave soon, and I would be on my own

LAN[   ]ACHSEN

Flüchtlings-Ausweis

zu Nummer

[ND/I/132082]

des Personalausweises der Britischen Zone
(nur gültig bei dessen gleichzeitiger Vorlage)

Wolfgang Samuel

Vor- und Zuname

(bei Frauen auch Mädchenname)

Samberg

(Wohnort - Aufnahmegemeinde)

Bxxxkkxx Bar. Trauen-V

(Straße und Haus-Nr.)

(Kreis)	Flüchtl.-Gruppe
Lüneburg	**A**
(Regierungsbezirk)	
Verlust des Ausweises ist sofort zu melden	Ausweisliste Nr. 574

My newly issued *Fluechtlings-Ausweis*, refugee pass, lists my home address as: 'bar. Trauen,' Barracks Trauen. Photo provided by the author.

again. Over dinner she told me that she and Leo wanted to get married. I was surprised to hear that she had finally said yes to someone.

"Leo started the application process. It is complex and tedious," she explained. "There are so many forms to fill out and interviews. I've come on this visit to get some of the paperwork started, since Fassberg is our permanent place of residence." We went to the Fassberg city hall the next day, and the first thing the clerk did was issue Mutti and me a Fluechtling's Ausweis, a refugee pass. I was puzzled.

Over four years after the war ended, we were still categorized as refugees, second-class citizens in my eyes, and they even gave us an identification card to certify our status. Mutti filled out papers for her marriage application certifying that she had no criminal record, had not been a member of the Nazi party, had no outstanding debts, and was a German citizen. The next morning she left again.

During the dreary winter months I kept busy with school, helping with the never-ending chores, and now and then seeing a movie in Munster-Lager. The potato farm where Opa Samuel worked would on Friday's, when the weather cooperated, hook an open wagon to the back of one of their tractors, and take their workers to Munster-Lager, to the *Kino*, the movie theater. They didn't mind if I came along. Other than that, in the long winter evenings, I sat at the kitchen table next to Opa, watching him smoke his pipe and repair baskets with willow reeds, baskets he had woven himself when he first came to the barracks in 1946. I looked at his gnarled hands. A Rumanian bullet had passed through one hand in another, long forgotten war. The light reflected off his silvery hair as he concentrated on his task. I tried to imagine the things he had experienced in life, all the decisions he had to make for himself and others. I learned he received a battlefield commission as a lieutenant in the Kaiser's army, but he wouldn't talk about war with me. After the Great War he and Oma had built a very nice, two-story house for themselves, furnished it, and then lost it all to another war. They never complained. Never. The two old people were instead planning to build a new house again. They didn't seem to need anyone else, just each other. They were truly self-reliant. Sitting at the table watching them, I thought that I wanted to be like them—independent and self-reliant.

Since my family had first come to the barracks in late 1946, little had changed. Of course the two neighbor women had died in 1947, one of syphilis, the other of a botched abortion. And Vera, my cousin, had come. The blonde Dutch girl had married her supervisor at the potato farm and left to start her own family. The two hulking Pash-

My father Willie, Oma and Opa Samuel, sitting in a meadow in front of their house, 1934. It was on the occasion when my father introduced my mother to his parents. Photo provided by the author.

mionka boys next door had succumbed to the good money they were told they could make as coal miners in the Ruhrgebiet after the Fassberg Air Base closed for a second time and they had lost their jobs again. Their parents and the younger boy stayed behind. Vera had a baby girl in 1949 and the father, a GCLO man, had moved in with her. Many more babies had been born to other women. The barracks Communist's wife was pregnant with her third child. There was no indication that he was going to join his comrades in the East. The "abortion lady" and her family moved out in March 1950. They rented a railroad car for their furniture. The next day the regularly scheduled passenger train came by and picked up the car. They climbed aboard, and with their belongings they were on their way to Cologne. A family in the barracks who needed more space moved into their empty apartment. When Fassberg Air Base had closed on the first of October, most people lost their jobs for the second or third time. They went to work on farms in nearby villages to earn a meager living. It was time to leave the barracks. It seemed that there was no permanent work for anyone in this poor region of Germany.

On April 2, 1950, Palm Sunday, my classmates and I, except for two who were not Evangelical Lutherans, were confirmed in St. Michael's Lutheran Church, located right next to our school. Once a week for the past year and a half, we had remained in school for two additional hours of religious instruction. Our pastor was a former U-boat chaplain. We studied the New Testament and learned the Ten Commandments. Mutti came from Fuerstenfeldbruck for the occasion, and my father came from Munster-Lager where he still worked for the British army. I bought myself a pin-striped dark blue suit with money Mutti and dad had given me, as well as new black shoes and a white shirt. Dad gave me a nice silk tie as a gift. The new clothes felt good once I had everything properly tied and buttoned up. It was a typical April day in north Germany—cool, overcast skies, but no rain. All three of us walked from the barracks to Fassberg. My mother and father walked together, deep in conversation the entire way. I walked behind them. I was proud and pleased that they both had come to be with me on a special occasion in my life. I felt this would probably be the last time I would see my mother and father walking together like this.

The church service was a plain Lutheran service. We were given permission to take our first Communion, to take bread and wine in honor of the Lord. The pastor delivered a lengthy sermon about the importance of confirmation to the church and to our own lives. He

My classmates and I were confirmed in this church on April 2, 1950. This was the beginning of a new phase of life for all of us, and few of us had any idea where the future would lead us. Photo provided by the author.

called out our names precisely and loudly, twenty-one boys and sixteen girls, to come forward and receive our confirmation certificates.

"Horst Boschatzki." Called first, according to the alphabet, a short, feisty boy. I liked Horst.

"Klaus Gerlach." A slight boy whose father was a pilot in the Luftwaffe and didn't make it. Klaus nearly always wore one of his father's flight caps.

"Eberhard Gundlach." Tall and blond, teeth as white and regular as those in a toothpaste advertisement. His father was a gardener, and in later years Eberhard would take over his father's nursery and significantly expand it.

"Franz Heidenreich." His father, Colonel Heidenreich, once commanded the 'Grosse Kampfflieger Schule'—combat training school—at Fassberg Air Base. He was later promoted to Major General and at war's end Fassberg was one of the air bases under his command.

"Arnim Krueger." My best friend and fellow refugee from the East. Arnim would apprentice with the local butcher and made that his profession for the rest of his life. He was one of the first among us to die.

"Alfred Mrotzek." The tall soccer goalie of the Fassberg Youth Soccer League.

"Gerd Paulini." Went to England, following his mother, who had married an English airman.

"Wolfgang Samuel." At the sound of my own name I was surprised, yet pleased to hear it called out. I walked forward in my new suit. The pastor's face was stern as he handed me my certificate of confirmation.

"Karl Toepritz." Really good in math. Became a streetcar driver in Hannover.

"Ursula Bleckert." Pretty and tall. Always made me blush when she spoke to me. I liked her.

"Helga Kretschmer." Arrogant and bright.

"Irene Schweitzer." Always smiling and friendly. Her father was a senior Luftwaffe officer at Fassberg Air Base, a combat flyer.

"Sigrid Wolf." The last in the alphabet. A tall and shy girl.

We were fourteen or fifteen years of age. I looked around at the thirty-six others, and I knew that our closeness was coming to an end. Where would we be next year? Where would we be in five years? What were our futures? I felt uneasy. School was coming to an end, my family was split up, and soon I would have to earn my own living. I was going to be totally on my own. The constants in my life—school and family—were melting away.

I became increasingly restless, worried about my future. I should get started arranging my life, I thought. I needed to learn something practical, a trade. It was April; school should be out later this month, and I didn't have a *Lehrstelle* yet. I spoke to my grandfather, and he agreed to accompany me to Celle, to register at the *Arbeitsamt* for an apprenticeship. Two days later, we rode our bicycles to

Celle. Opa had always been a man of his word, and he did everything he could to help me find a place to learn a useful trade. I thought that maybe learning to be an electrician, a metal worker, or even a plumber would be useful. But there was nothing of that sort available, not in Fassberg and not even in Celle, a much larger town. Only two positions were offered me by the *Arbeitsamt*—one as a carpenter's apprentice at a small furniture manufacturer in Hermansburg, a smallish town not far from Fassberg, and the other as a baker's apprentice in Hannover. I wanted to get away to a city. Opa said we would look at both positions. The *Arbeitsamt* made appointments for us to meet with each of the two masters, who were qualified and authorized to train apprentices in their respective trades. Since Hermansburg was the closest we went there first. I didn't think much of going there, no matter how nice the apprenticeship might be. I wanted to get away from the barracks, from the memories of my past, and live in a completely new place. On the appointed day Opa and I took the train to Hannover to meet with Herr Franz Krampe of the Rheinische Baeckerei at Detmold Strasse 1. The meeting went well and I agreed to start my apprenticeship on April 30. On the way home I asked Opa, "What do you think?"

"I don't know Wolfgang," he replied honestly. "Krampe wants you pretty badly, and there isn't really anything else available right now. I suggest you take it. Three years isn't that long. You'll survive." As soon as Oma found out that I was going to be a baker's apprentice, she started talking up the bakery business. She even brought up a relative who had been a successful baker in the past.

On our last day of school, we were more subdued than normal. We sat down at our usual positions, knowing it would be for the last time. Herr Soffner, our homeroom teacher and school principal, said a few words. And after an hour we went home. There was no ceremony, no names were read out loud, no certificates presented. We were finished. I found the ending of our schooling to be abrupt, as if the state was embarrassed and glad to be rid of us, the war children.

On our last day of school we had a class photo taken. The girls dressed in their finest; the boys wore the shabby clothing we always had worn. Top row, second from left, my close friend, Arnim Krueger. Top row, second from right, Wolfgang Samuel. Middle row, second from right, Wolfgang Luthmer. Herr Soffner, our principal and homeroom teacher, standing second row right. Photo provided by the author.

The following day, Saturday, the girls had planned a party for us and our teachers. They arranged the tables in a larger classroom than our own—ours was a converted basement room—in a U-shape, with Herr Soffner sitting in the middle at the head table. The girls had baked cakes and fancy *Torten*, and served real coffee. We ate cake, drank coffee, and smiled at each other. But the girls had a surprise for us boys. They had sat down and together come up with a short poem about each one of us boys—and ceremoniously read their compositions to the sound of embarrassed laughter and genuine applause. I was surprised at their talent. Their little act of compassion brought a more up-beat end to our school experience.

The apprenticeship in Hannover was a six-day, fourteen-hour job, from two in the morning until four in the afternoon. My room turned out to be a barely renovated room in an adjacent bombed-out

My mother Hedy and Leo in 1950 in Fuerstenfeldbruck. Leo wears his new Air Force blues. Photo provided by the author.

building, with only cold running water and no heat. I was relieved when one day I received a letter from my mother asking me to come down to Fuerstenfeldbruck. Herr Krampe reluctantly let me go. Halfway through my stay Mutti asked me if I would accompany her to the United States when Leo got transferred back home. "I really don't want to go if you won't come along, Wolfgang. I would be too alone without you. Ingrid won't come, I've already spoken to her. She wants to stay with her father."

I was stunned by her request. I thought I was on my own once I started my apprenticeship in Hannover. Her request suddenly transformed a dreary future into one of sunshine and endless possibilities. Maybe I can fly with the men of the Berlin airlift after all? Trying to sound composed, which I was not, I said, "Of course I will go with you." Leo made an appointment for me at the air base hospital. The sign over the entrance, when we got there, read :36th Medical Group, Fuerstenfeldbruck Air Force Base." In later years I would fly with the 36th Tactical Fighter Wing, then at Bitburg Air Base, in the Eifel mountains. A friendly nurse took me by the hand. She motioned for me to remove my shirt. "*Hemd aus ziehen*," she said laughing loudly at the sound of her German. I removed my shirt and she pressed my chest against a glass plate. "*Nicht Atmen*," she said as she took an X-ray of my lungs. Then she took blood from my arm, and I had to leave a urine sample. An American doctor in an officer's uniform covered loosely by a white coat listened to my lungs and heart and asked several questions which I didn't understand. Leo gave him the answers he wanted to hear. And then we were finished.

When Sunday came, Mutti and Leo walked me to the train station early in the morning. I watched the same beautiful countryside glide past that I had seen a week earlier. The bombed-out cities with their ruined houses and churches stood unchanged. Wooden scaffolding clung to the exterior of some ruins. Something new was about to arise from the ashes of our awful past. It was a start, even if it would take fifty years to finish. I suddenly felt that I had a real future as well, in a new land that I knew very little about. But it was, as my father had told me many times, "the land of unlimited opportunities." I believed it would be a totally new beginning for me—I would no longer be a *Fluechtling*, a refugee, and I didn't have to be a baker for the rest of my life, after all.

Hedy, Leo, and I crossed the Atlantic in January of 1951. It was a very stormy voyage. Most of the passengers were seasick, but not I. I showed up for every meal and usually had seconds. I had not seen so much wonderful food in years. After a while the servers knew me—the German kid who eats everything and always takes seconds. They smiled when they saw me coming down the line. With a stop at Southampton, England, the voyage lasted a total of eleven days. Two days after my sixteenth birthday we arrived in New York, and after a day's long bus ride arrived in my new hometown of Denver, Colorado. I

The old railroad tracks, laid in the early 1930s, on which the coal for Berlin was brought into Fassberg Air Base in 1948, were still there when I visited the airfield in 2002. A reminder of my own past. Photo provided by the author.

had a dream, to fly with the men of the Berlin airlift who had been so inspirational to me. I spoke no English when I came to Denver, only the usual gibberish children acquire. I managed to cope and graduated from East High school in 1953, then joined the US Air Force as an enlisted man, which qualified me for the Korean War GI Bill, which I later used to put myself through college, graduating in 1960. While stationed in England in 1956, I returned to Fassberg to visit my old school. Herr Soffner was still there. I wore my American uniform, and our meeting was warm and cordial. In 1960 I entered flight training. In the following years I flew strategic reconnaissance against the Soviet Union and eventually in 1968 found myself in Thailand flying combat against North Vietnam. I was a child of war, and here I was back in it again, this time as an active combatant, not an innocent child.

In 1970, after being assigned to Headquarters USAFE in Wiesbaden, Germany, following my Vietnam combat tour of duty, I did

My dear grandparents Wilhelm and Anna Samuel, when I visited them in Elmpt/
Niederrhein near the Dutch border in 1956. Opa told me when we still lived in the
barracks in Trauen that he would build a house again. We are standing in front of
the small house he built for Oma; then he built a larger, two-story house for my
father Willie and his family to live in. Willie worked at RAF Brueggen until his retirement. Today, my half-brother Gerhard and his family live in the house Opa built.
Photo provided by the author.

some of my flying with the 36th Tactical Fighter Wing at Bitburg Air
Base. On my first flight out of Bitburg I recalled that X-ray experience in Fuerstenfeldbruck, when the 36th Tactical Fighter Bomber
Wing was stationed there. Subsequently assigned as an exchange
officer to the 15th Generalstabslehrgang of the newly created Luftwaffe in Hamburg-Blankenese, I took the opportunity with my family
to return to Fassberg. And as I drove up Poitzenerstrasse I passed a
large nursery, a man working out front. I stopped, and to my great
surprise it was my old *Schulkamerad*, school friend, Eberhard Gund-

lach. I made many return visits meeting with Eberhard, Horst Boschatzki, Irene Schweitzer, and Renate Panthen. I wasn't surprised that most of my classmates no longer resided in Fassberg, but had relocated where they found employment or family took them, one to England, another to Australia,

One of my Generalstabslehrgang's classmates from 1973–1975 at Hamburg-Blankenese gained me permission to visit Fassberg Air Base, now a Luftwaffe training base, as it was at its inception in the mid-1930s. The old railroad tracks were still there where coal trains once arrived to light and heat West Berlin. I went into the hangar where at one time Leo Ferguson was billeted and where I took my first hot shower years ago. I looked at the empty ramps once filled with C-47 and C-54 transports and in my mind I saw it all again the way it was in those hope-filled days when I was still a *Fluechtling*, a refugee, with an uncertain future, living in a squalid camp adjacent to the Fassberg airfield. I returned to Trauen, to the site where the barracks once stood. They had been razed of course and a young pine forest covered the site. I looked for any signs of my past—and I found it in some small currant bushes that my grandmother Anna Samuel once planted, and that refused to die when the site was leveled. No one else had these bushes in their garden plots, so it felt for me as if my dear, courageous, and never complaining grandmother was here again with her beloved grandson—reaching out, in a different way. The tears I shed that moment of discovery were tears of the boy I once was.

10

The Other Side of
Courage and Compassion

On July 17, after several missions, he visited Berlin as a passenger hoping to take movies of the city. While walking near the barbed wire fence off the end of the Tempelhof runway, he noticed children watching the airplanes. These German children acted differently from other children, Halvorsen noted, as they did not ask for candy or gum—expecting nothing, they asked for nothing. He divided among them the only two sticks of gum he had left, and then made a rash promise: if they returned to the fence, Halvorsen told the kids, he would drop gum and candy from his airplane.
—**Roger G. Miller,** *To Save a City*

On the other side of the border between East and West, in the city of Berlin, eventually saved from an ugly fate by the flyers from Fassberg, Celle, Frankfurt, and Wiesbaden, lived women and children who in blind faith believed that those incredible men in their flying machines were going to deliver the peace they so fervently prayed for. Berlin, like Fassberg, Wiesbaden, and Frankfurt, was home to wives and families of American, French, and British military men and foreign service personnel stationed in the city. The women knew all too well—as General Bradley did when he reassigned his son-in-law out of the city to get his daughter to a safer place, just in case things didn't work out—that things could turn ugly quickly. Bradley remembered all too well what happened in Berlin when the war came to its ugly end, the indiscriminate killing and rape of young girls and women. He didn't want to take a chance with his daughter. Yet, all the others had no such options available to them and stayed behind, knowing that if things didn't work out. . . . They had faith that things would turn out as promised. Faith, by definition, is believing in something or someone when there is no proof to back up your beliefs. You just believe that the expected promise will be delivered. There was no precedent for what the Western Allies had just come up with—an airlift to not only supply the basic needs of their own garrisons, but to do the same for over two million German residents of the western sectors of the city of Berlin. The children of Berlin, gaunt and hungry, dressed in hand-me-downs or worse, standing on the heaps of rubble watching the "Candy Bombers" flying into Tempelhof, knew for sure that those flyers would not let them down.

Berlin in 1948 was mostly a devastated wasteland of street after street of bombed-out houses. People lived in the ruins of a once great European city, which at this time was no more. I remember in February 1945, around my tenth birthday, the one thousand bomber raids of the 8th Air Force. Berlin and its suburbs comprised a huge area of houses, shops, factories, and parks. But in time the raids of the magnitude that I recall leveled much of the city, street by street. My mom and I left the city before the onslaught of the Russian armies, which destroyed much of what had not been leveled by the Army Air Forces and the RAF. On a 1947 visit then Congressman Richard Nixon was escorted by General Lucius D. Clay, the military governor of the American occupation zone and Western sector of Berlin. In a few words quoted in Jean Edward Smith's biography of the general, Clay summarized what things were like: "We found thousands of families huddled in the debris of buildings and in bunkers. "There

was a critical shortage of food, and thin faced, half-dressed children approached, not to beg but to sell their fathers' war medals or to trade them for something to eat. Nixon was profoundly moved by the spirit of the children who would not beg," There was no thriving *Kurfuerstendam* then where one could go shopping, sit and have tea or coffee; there was only darkness, cold, and memories of an ugly past.

For the women who chose to accompany their husbands to Berlin, social life was indeed extremely limited and whatever life they had, they largely came up with on their own. One encouragement for the wives throughout this difficult period, especially in the dark days of the winter of 1948 to 1949, was to see American and British transports, first smaller C-47s and Dakotas, later the larger, four-engine C-54s, fly into Berlin day after day, hour after hour. Delivering not only food, but also coal to provide heat and light for suffering Berliners. Among those flyers was one who was touched by the plight of the children of Berlin and wanted to do something about it. He did and would put a human face on the entire Berlin airlift effort,

and in many ways helped transition the German people from former enemies to just people in need of help. His name was First Lieutenant Gail Halvorsen.

Gail was based in Alabama and on July 10, 1948, flew a C-54 from Brookley Air Force Base to Frankfurt's Rhein-Main Air Base. On July 12, only two days after leaving Brookley, Gail flew his first load of food into Berlin. As he made his approach into Templehof airfield that day, and in subsequent days, he noticed children standing on mounds of rubble watching him come in for a landing. It touched his heart. Gail didn't see the ruble, he only saw the children—thin faced, poorly clothed. On July 18 Gail had an opportunity to come face to face with those children, and he made a decision to put a smile on their thin faces. The following day he dropped three makeshift parachutes, handkerchiefs filled with candy bars and gum, to the children below. His copilot and flight engineer quickly became part of this effort, although they were a bit uneasy how this unauthorized activity on their part would be received by higher-ups once it became known.

Gail Halvorsen and I at a Berlin Airlift Veterans Association reunion in Dayton, Ohio. I had met Gail in 1970 when by chance we were seatmates on a Pan American Airlines flight from Frankfurt to Berlin. Pan Am, as it was generally referred to, and BEA, British European Airways, had the concessions to provide civilian air travel to and from Berlin. Halvorsen was a colonel and commanded the Air Force Berlin contingent at the time. I was a major, a staff officer, at HQ USAFE at Lindsey Air Station in Wiesbaden. Photo provided by the author.

On days to follow other flyers joined in, dropping more para-chutes filled with candy. This unusual act of compassion soon made its way up the chain of command, and two weeks after Gail dropped his first makeshift parachute, he stood in front of his squadron com-mander explaining himself. Soon Major General William Tunner, overall airlift commander, heard of what Lieutenant Halvorsen had done—and he liked it. Operation Little Vittles was born and the small handkerchief candy drop turned into a massive operation delivering tons of candy to the children of Berlin—not only candy, but hope for a better future. In April 1949, soon after the Easter Parade success, General Hoyt Vandenberg, the second chief of staff of the newly

Colonel Wolfgang W. Samuel, USAF (Ret.), author, Colonel Gail Halvorsen, USAF (Ret.), and Joan Powers, my wife, in 2019 at the National Air and Space Museum Udvar Hazy Center in Chantilly, Virginia. Gail, at age ninety-eight, is wearing the *Bundesverdienstkreuz* around his neck awarded him by the German government in recognition of Operation Little Vittles, initiated by Gail during the Berlin airlift of 1948–1949. We are standing behind the space shuttle Discovery at Udvar Hazy. Photo provided by the author.

created United States Air Force, announced that the Little Vittles originator, Lieutenant Gail Halvorsen, had been selected to receive the prestigious Cheney Award for 1948. Lieutenant Halvorsen had expected nothing in return for his selfless, compassionate act. The Cheney Award is presented by the United States Air Force in memory of First Lieutenant William H. Cheney who was killed in an aerial collision over Foggia, Italy, on January 20, 1918. Established in 1927, the award is for an act of valor, extreme fortitude, or self-sacrifice in a humanitarian effort performed in connection with aircraft, but not necessarily of a military nature.

Gail Halvorsen's candy drops proved to be an inspiration to the wives of Berlin's senior Allied military and foreign service establishment, and they decided to support the ongoing airlift in the best way they knew how. Their choice was a cookbook for which each of them submitted a recipe. They were imaginative, signing their respective recipes, even adding a cartoon at times and a clever insight or recollection. I may mention that many, if not most, had German maids and cooks. I recall when assigned my quarters in base housing in 1970 in Wiesbaden, Germany, then the location of Headquarters USAFE, each apartment in my housing development, built between 1946 and 1948, had maids' quarters on the upper level of the two-story apartment houses, built right under the traditional German steep roofs. So, having a maid for American officers' families stationed in Germany at this time was considered normal, and quarters were built to accommodate such help.

The cover of the cookbook reflected the ongoing airlift—food for the hungry.

It is quite an imaginative cover using a bird analogy, depicting the Soviets, from their nest, trying to cut down the branch on which the Allies—French, British, American, and West Berliners—had their nest, awaiting to be fed, like birds feeding their young hatchlings. Mrs Marjorie Clay, the wife of General Lucius D. Clay, who then was the governor of Trizonia (the British, French, and American occupation zones) and Commander in Chief of the European Command, signed the dedication and introduction to the cookbook.

There are over ninety recipes in this delightful cookbook, although I have to admit some of them are on the somewhat strange side. However, they are reflective of the times, not so much of Berlin, but of the relative simplicity of life in the United States of the 1940s, where after all most of the women came from. The *Operation Vittles Cook Book* came out in January 1949, during the most difficult period of the Berlin airlift. I very much enjoyed reading the little snippets of life added at the beginning of each recipe—I am sure you will too.

OPERATION

VITTLES

COOK BOOK

compiled by

THE AMERICAN WOMEN

in

BLOCKADED BERLIN

January 1949

Dedicated to the happy group of wives who attempted to obtain American meals by slaying the dragons of language, old utensils, ovens sans thermometers, conflicting opinions, etc., ad infinitum . . . and to the many excellent cooks who bore with the puzzling variety in the American diet — the endless series of *"Immer was neu ist!"*

Our joy that we have persuaded a few Germans to the edibility of corn, which they had always thought was intended for horses and American Indians, is somewhat diminished when we consider the small proportion thus influenced.

MARY'S CORNBREAD

1¼ C flour
¾ C cornmeal
2 T sugar
2½ t baking powder
½ t salt
1 C milk
1 egg (slightly beaten)
2 T shortening (melted)

Sift dry ingredients together. Add milk to egg. Add to flour mixture. Add shortening. Pour into greased baking dish. Bake.

Oven: 350°   Time: 25 minutes

Marian McCurdy

Everyone knows the first stock in trade of the German black-market is the cigarette, so it was with considerable shock that one mother heard her little three-year-old sweetly ask for two. On inquiry, she wanted the cigarettes for "the nice man who cleans our mice cage at school."

MOLASSES COOKIES

1 C butter
1 C brown sugar
1 C sugar
1 C molasses
½ t cinnamon
1 t salt
1 T ginger
2 eggs (well-beaten)
5 C flour
2 t soda

Heat first 7 ingredients together, just warm. Cool. Add eggs. Mix. Sift flour with soda and add, mixing well. Shape in rolls, wrap in wax paper. Refrigerate until cold. Slice thin and bake.

Oven: 350°

Mae Agnes Honan

21

The maid had been instructed to prepare a plate of hors d'oeuvres —half on bread and half on crackers. Time to serve and in came a platter of sandwiches, crackers on top—bread below! But the hors d'oeuvre to end all same was dreamed up by a cook who felt her favorite guest deserved something special—sweet gherkins sliced lengthwise, each topped with a maraschino cherry!

CHEESE STICKS

1 C   shortening

1 C   flour

1 C   cheese (grated)

pinch of salt

Mix thoroughly and roll very thin. Cut in strips and bake on ungreased baking sheet.

Oven: 450°   Time: 15 minutes

Dorothy A Welch

32

The battle between electricity cut-offs and the unfinished roast has often taken a roast from an oven in one sector to the oven of another where the electricity was still on. We think a lamb roast established the record when it went in and out to a total of 22 hours baking and traveling time.

SHASHLIK (Poland)

3 lbs. mutton fillet

¾ lb. bacon

3 onions (medium size)

2 C flour

salt and pepper

Cut meat into 1½ inch pieces, ½ inch thick. Pound to flatten. Cut bacon in squares and slice onions. Put in succession on skewers (meat, bacon, onion, etc.). Roll each filled skewer in flour, then sprinkle with seasonings. Broil over open fire or on hot frying pan for 15 minutes. (Sliced fresh mushrooms may also be used; meat, mushroom, bacon, onion.)

Elizabeth Randolph Betts

43

VEGETABLES

The necessity-born German trick of "cooking" foods under the bed covers was quickly adopted by us Berlin Americans when the blockade cut our electricity down to a few short hours daily. Most common dish to be bedded down for the finishing process was rice, but we tried it with great success on roasts and favorite casseroles.

CORN PUDDING

¼ C milk

½ t salt

2 eggs (beaten)

¼ green pepper (chopped)

1 can cream style corn

2 T butter

Add milk and salt to eggs. Mix. Add green pepper and corn. Mix well. Place in buttered baking dish, dot with butter. Bake.

Oven: 350°   Time: 40 minutes

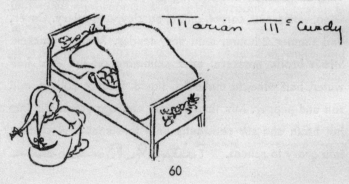

Marian McCurdy

60

The young British wife of a G.I. had given birth to her first son at our 279th Station Hospital. In her joy she informed the other new American mothers, "My son can never be king of England but he can be President of the United States!"

SQUASH RING

2 C steamed, strained squash

2 T butter (melted)

1 egg (beaten)

1 T chopped parsley

1 t minced onion

⅓ C bread crumbs (fine)

salt and pepper

Mix all ingredients together. Put in greased mold. Bake. Unmold to serve. (Good with white cheese sauce.)

Oven: 350°   Time: 25 minutes

Anne M. Litchfield

68

The Potato was first introduced to the skeptical Germans by the father of Frederick the Great. When his subjects refused to eat the strange American food, the king arranged a public viewing of himself at table eating an enormous plate of the worthy vegetable. From then on, the potato gained popularity until today it is indeed the mainstay of the German diet.

QUICK BROWN GRAVY

1   can cream of mushroom soup
1   can consomme
3   T   flour
½   C   water
1   t   Kitchen Bouquet

Mix soup and consomme. Mix flour, water and Kitchen Bouquet. Heat soup, add flour mixture slowly and simmer for 10 minutes.

Marjorie G Ward

88

MISCELLANEOUS

We have each, in turn, been introduced at Christmas time to the nice old German custom of Advent candles. Four Sundays before Christmas, a wreath is placed in a prominent spot and on it stand four candles. The first Sunday only one candle is burned, the second two, and so on until Christmas.

OLD ENGLISH MINCEMEAT

1	lb.	beef suet (chopped fine)
6	C	apples (chopped fine)
3	C	seeded raisins
2½	C	Sultana raisins
2⅜	C	currants
1½	C	ground almonds
3½	C	sugar
3	C	candied lemon peel (chopped)

juice of 2 oranges

rind of 1 lemon

juice of 2 lemons

1	t	nutmeg
2	T	allspice
½	C	brandy

Alice Davisson

89

Most of our billets, we found on arrival, were equipped with refrigerators which were usually in working order. Sadly, though, they were always half-empty and it took long months to teach the Germans the wide variety of foods which we considered better preserved by refrigeration.

FRENCH DRESSING

½ C sugar

1 t paprika

1 t salt

1 T dry mustard

1 C salad oil

1 C vinegar

1 can tomato soup

1 T chili sauce

1 T Worcestershire sauce

juice of 1 lemon

Mix dry ingredients together. Put remaining ingredients in quart jar. Add dry mixture. Shake well and keep in refrigerator.

Amount: 1 quart

Elizabeth H. Agniel

The Berlin Germans were beginning to realize that Operation Vittles would successfully supply their needs, and to thrill to the personal import of each winged cargo as it came in sight, when the ragged youngsters playing on the streets below dubbed the planes, realistically, "Noodle Bombers."

HURRY-UP SUPPER DISH

1   package noodles

½ C   butter (melted to golden brown)

2 C   cottage cheese

⅓ C   sugar and cinnamon (half and half)

Cook noodles and drain. Mix with butter. Put noodles on platter. Place layer of cottage cheese on noodles. Sprinkle with sugar-cinnamon mixture.

Evelyn Panuck

82

NO TIME AT ALL

Ah, but the sight of the first chimney sweep at our door! Tall silk hat, soot-blackened face, paraphernalia fastened wherever possible, and, of course, the bicycle. The Schornsteinfeger is necessary in Germany, where soft coal is burned, and everyone believes he brings good luck.

QUICK-CHANGE SOUP

Clear soup		Cream soup
4 T	cream of wheat	½ C
1 T	butter	4 T
5 C	water	4 C
6	bouillon cubes	—
—	cream	½ C
—	salt	½ t
2 T	chopped parsley	2 T

Brown cream of wheat in butter, stirring constantly. Slowly add boiling water. For clear soup keep boiling and add bouillon cubes, stirring until dissolved. For cream soup boil 5 minutes, remove from stove, add cream and salt. Pour into soup dishes, sprinkle with parsley and serve.

Beryl R. Clarke

Ten years ago an American family stationed in Berlin sent their children to the Gertrauden-Schule in Berlin-Dahlem. By strange coincidence, the same children are attending the same school, which, however, is now American.

PTA DOUGHNUTS

¼　C　shortening

⅔　C　sugar

1　t　salt

3　　eggs (beaten)

¾　C　milk

1　t　vanilla

2⅞　C　flour

6　t　baking powder

Cream shortening, sugar and salt. Add eggs and beat until smooth. Add milk and vanilla. Sift flour with baking powder three times. Add, beating well. Roll out on floured board until ½ inch thick. Cut with doughnut cutter. Fry in deep fat (360° hot) until brown.

Esther Froistad

5

Our men like the old German recipe for the perfect woman: "Kinder, Kirche, Küche,"—Children, Church, Kitchen.

LADY FINGERS

3   eggs (separate 3 whites; 2 yolks; 1 yolk un-used)
5   T   sifted powdered sugar
¼   t   salt
½   t   vanilla
5   T   sifted cake flour
powdered sugar for dusting

Beat egg whites until stiff and fold in sugar. Beat yolks until thick. Add salt and vanilla and fold into white mixture. Fold in flour. Cover baking sheet with brown paper. With pastry tube, shape each lady finger about 4 inches long and 1 inch wide. Bake. Remove from paper with knife and put together in pairs while still warm. Lay on waxed paper. Dust with powdered sugar.

Oven: 350°   Time: 12 minutes

Evelyn Panuch

20

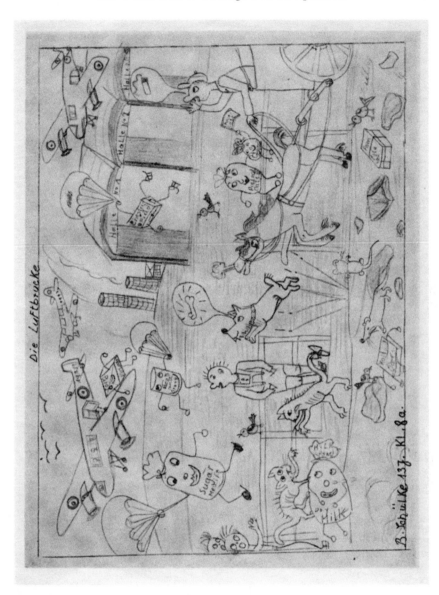

This Berlin airlift scenario was a creation of a thirteen-year-old eighth-grade student in a Berlin school. I love the dog dreaming of receiving a bone to chew on.

The aircraft is called by its student creator Butterflyer; below is a depiction of the trucks which distribute the food the youngsters dreamed about.

The ladies of the Berlin airlift included several drawings from German schoolchildren in their cookbook. A child's perception of the world around it is usually very honest and fact driven—they try to represent the world they experience and are a part of in childlike innocence. The children whose graphics are shown were eighth and ninth graders, fourteen to fifteen years old, my age at that time. The airplane is in every picture but one—not planes dropping bombs, but planes providing food and hope for a better life.

Gail Halvorsen showed compassion for the children of Berlin and humanized the airlift. The wives of American servicemen and diplomats stationed in Berlin in their own way, through a cookbook, memorialized the airlift, which embodied their own hopes for a better future. There was a third whose efforts were all encompassing like Gail's and the American Wives of Berlin—Jake Schuffert. Not to include Jake in any anthology would be remiss. Jake was a WWII B-24 radio operator, shot down over Yugoslavia. He survived. At war's end Jake stayed on wearing an Army Air Forces uniform. Come the Berlin airlift, they only needed pilots and flight engineers, not radio operators. So Jake offered his services to the *Airlift Times* as a cartoonist. The *Times* was a paper published by the Air Force for airlift personnel. Jake Schuffert's cartoons captured the very spirit of the Berlin airlift, the can-do attitude of the flyers and of everyone involved in one way or another. So I will end this chapter with a select few of Schuffert's cartoons.

"HE'S THE NEW NOSE AND THROAT SPECIALIST FOR THE COAL FLIERS, SIR!!"

"SIR, MY NAME'S PFC CELLE, I WANT A TRANSFER—"

11

The World after the Berlin Airlift

Clay responded (to Ernst Reuter, mayor of Berlin): "The end of the blockade does not merely mean that trains and trucks are moving again. It has a deeper significance. The people of Berlin have earned their right to freedom and to be accepted by those who love freedom everywhere." Clay's translator, Robert Lochner, was stunned when he looked over at the man who had been compared to a Roman emperor. Lucius Clay was crying.
—**Richard Reeves**, *Daring Young Men*

The Berlin airlift is unique in military history as a major confrontation between military powers where not a bullet was fired to determine the outcome. Although there was significant friction between the United States and the Soviet Union before 1948, after the Berlin airlift ended in 1949 the Soviet Union's westward expansion came to an abrupt halt. From now on it became an issue for the Soviets to hang on to what they had; forty years of Cold War ensued. In the end, it proved to be a losing battle for the Soviet leadership. Berlin, more than any other factor, probably contributed to the Soviet Union's demise. Berlin became a universal symbol of freedom, a thorn in the side of the Soviets. In a speech given in West Berlin in June 1987 by then President Ronald Reagan he pointedly asked Mr. Gorbachev to "tear down this wall," referring to the Berlin Wall dividing the city to keep East Germans from escaping to the West. Within a brief few years not only did the wall come down, but the Soviet Union itself met an inglorious end.

As early as April 8, 1949, while the Berlin airlift was in full swing, a Tripartite Agreement was signed on the creation of the Federal Republic of Germany. Only a few weeks later, on May 21, 1949, the German Federal Republic was established. Without the Soviet grab for Berlin, it is doubtful the Western Allies would have moved on this issue with such speed. The most important consequence of the Soviet blockade of Berlin was undoubtedly the formation of the North Atlantic Treaty Organization, NATO. The treaty became effective on August 24, 1949. President Truman stepped right into the newly assumed responsibilities and on October 6, 1949, signed the Mutual Defense Assistance Act authorizing American aid to NATO members. Under the authority of this act, some of the Berlin airlift C-47 transports and those of the former EATS, European Air Transport Service, found their way into the military arsenals of NATO members from Denmark and Norway to Greece and Turkey.

NATO, as an entity, asserted itself promptly when the Council of Foreign Ministers, on September 19, 1950, declared that any attack upon the German Federal Republic or upon West Berlin was considered an attack upon themselves. How things had changed for the outlook of the Soviet Union in such a brief period of time. And, like putting a cherry as a finishing touch on an ice cream sundae, on December 18, 1950, General Dwight D. Eisenhower was appointed Supreme Allied Commander Europe, SACEUR. General Eisenhower would serve in that capacity until April 28, 1952, when he resigned to eventually accept the Republican nomination for president. He was replaced on May 30, 1952, by General Matthew B. Ridgeway, who had fought under Eisenhower's command in Europe, later assumed command of the 8th US Army in Korea and became Supreme Commander Far East after President Truman relieved General MacAr-

"—AND FURTHERMORE, I DIDN'T WANT THAT TANK REFUELED ANYHOW!!"

"IF IT WASN'T FOR THE AIRLIFT,
CLEMENTINE WOULD HAVE STARVED TO DEATH!!"

thur of command. Both Eisenhower and Ridgeway were the best and the brightest of America's military heritage.

Only four years earlier the Soviet Union's leadership considered much of Europe ready for the picking, and certainly Berlin seemed an easy first. How quickly things changed with this miscalculation, brought about by the stunning success of the Berlin airlift flyers, an idea that was broached by a mid-level British officer and doubted to succeed at the highest levels of the US Air Force and by President Truman's closest advisers. The little town of Fassberg, built for war in 1935, played a significant part in this role reversal thirteen years later, turning Fassberg Air Base into a beacon of freedom instead.

Less than a year after the end of the Berlin airlift, the United States was involved in a military confrontation in Korea, which revealed significant weaknesses in American military preparedness. Across the board the United States began to reconstitute its military capabilities. NATO, and especially the United States, realized early on, to be effective, there had to be a German contribution. On May 5, 1955, the occupation of West Germany ended, and days later the Federal Republic of Germany became a NATO member.

The Berlin airlift not only preserved the freedom of a city, but acted as a catalyst in bringing the West—England, France, and the United States—together as an entity to respond to aggression. And West Germany, the Federal Republic of Germany, in the process transitioned from an occupied enemy country to that of a fledgling democracy, an idea that had failed miserably after World War I and led to Hitler seizing power in 1933 only to lead the world into a brutal and gruesome war. The small town of Fassberg no longer had to worry about its existence; its airfield would become an integral part of the Allied defense structure for years to come. And an amazing thing had happened to this small town, a little town built for war. It suddenly had become a pillar for peace. Something its Nazi creators could have never imagined.

However, there was a cost exacted. Forty British, thirty-one Americans and five Germans lost their lives in varied accidents while performing airlift-related duties. Others were killed, such as the seven German children, part of a *Kindertransport* effort, who were passengers in a British Dakota which crashed on January 24, 1949, in the Russian zone of occupation. The beginning for the airlift started on a sour note. In July and August 1948 four C-47 aircraft were lost including eight crew members and one Department of the Army civilian. One of the early C-54 crashes occurred on December 5, 1948, when an aircraft piloted by Captain Billy Phelps, assisted by copilot First Lieutenant Willis Hargis and Technical Sergeant Lloyd Wells, the flight engineer, crashed near the Trauen refugee camp where I lived at the time as a young teenager. For me it was a heartbreaking experience when I went to visit the crash site. Only three years earlier American B-17 bombers had terrified me when I lived in the city of Berlin, and now, these same men were dying to save Berlin. I wanted to know more about these Americans, wanted to be like them, wear their uniform when I grew up, fly with them. But I knew that would never happen. No matter what the future held for me, I knew that I would never forget these men. I would always remember their self-less humanity, of caring for the very people who were their enemies only three years earlier.

A second C-54 based at RAF Fassberg crashed on January 18, 1949, with the loss of one of its pilots, First Lieutenant Robert P. Weaver. There were only twelve fatal US accidents resulting in the loss of thirty-one American lives in a total of 586,901 flying hours. Twenty-two C-47/C-54 aircraft were destroyed. It was an amazing flight safety record flown in all kinds of weather, without interruption, day and night, over a period of fifteen months.

In raw numbers the airlift was a stunning achievement. In 277,569 flights by both American and British aircraft, 2,325,510 tons of food and coal was delivered to the besieged city. The American contribution under Operation Vittles totaled 1,783,573 short tons, while the British under Operation Plainfare delivered 541,937 tons of coal, food, and miscellaneous cargo. The United States Air Force also learned an important lesson. Relying on modified airliners such as the C-47, C-54, and later on the C-97 and C-121was not an approach that guaranteed that strategic and tactical airlift needs could be met. In addition, airlift could not be viewed as an additional duty such as during the Berlin airlift when pilots and flight engineers with varied backgrounds were randomly assigned to fly the mission. The transition to a Military Air Transport Service, MATS, totally dedicated to providing strategic airlift, would take years, as did the development of a viable tactical airlift capability. Aircraft such as the C-130A in the late 1950s led the way on the tactical side, and on the strategic airlift side it was the huge C-124, nicknamed Old Shaky by its crews, which would be augmented by the C-133, which then led to the all jet C-141 and C-5 during the Vietnam War years and the C-17 of today. The Berlin airlift was a turning point away from World War II to the future which had changed significantly in terms of international relations and the advent of new and revolutionary technologies.

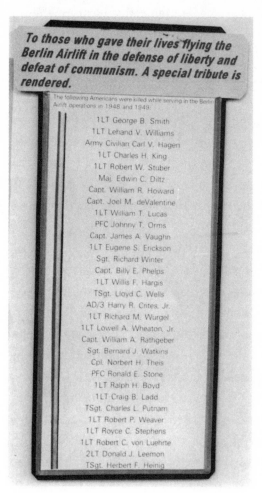

To those who gave their lives flying the Berlin Airlift in the defense of liberty and defeat of communism. A special tribute is rendered.

The following Americans were killed while serving in the Berlin Airlift operations in 1948 and 1949:

1LT George B. Smith
1LT Lehand V. Williams
Army Civilian Carl V. Hagen
1LT Charles H. King
1LT Robert W. Stuber
Maj. Edwin C. Diltz
Capt. William R. Howard
Capt. Joel M. deValentine
1LT William T. Lucas
PFC Johnny T. Orms
Capt. James A. Vaughn
1LT Eugene S. Erickson
Sgt. Richard Winter
Capt. Billy E. Phelps
1LT Willis F. Hargis
TSgt. Lloyd C. Wells
AD/3 Harry R. Crites, Jr.
1LT Richard M. Wurgel
1LT Lowell A. Wheaton, Jr.
Capt. William A. Rathgeber
Sgt. Bernard J. Watkins
Cpl. Norbert H. Theis
PFC Ronald E. Stone
1LT Ralph H. Boyd
1LT Craig B. Ladd
TSgt. Charles L. Putnam
1LT Robert P. Weaver
1LT Royce C. Stephens
1LT Robert C. von Luehrte
2LT Donald J. Leemon
TSgt. Herbert F. Heinig

A memorial panel of the Berlin Airlift Association commemorating the Americans who lost their lives in the Berlin Airlift of 1948–1949. Photo courtesy of the author.

12

A Town Trying to Stay Alive after the End of the *Luftbruecke*

One could raise the question: Did the Cold War assure the future of Fassberg? Was it not due to the political developments in the summer of 1948 which pointed out the importance of the airfield? Thereby assuring the survival of Fassberg?
—**Christoph M. Glombek,** *Chronik der Gemeinde Fassberg*

December 1949 in Fassberg was cold and miserable, as I remember all too well. The streets were empty. There were no more raucous Americans partying until late in Mom's Place. Mom's Place closed down as did everything else that had come to life when the Americans arrived. The moneychangers and the men who set up their tables along the road leading to the main gate, selling gadgets and trinkets, were gone. As were the girls of the night, the Veronikas, who hung around the airfield's gate waiting to be picked up. They were not bad girls, mostly girls come on hard times who tried their best to make a living, maybe even marry one of their American nighttime friends. Most of all it was very quiet around Fassberg—there was no more airplane noise. That was not a good sign for the future.

What remained behind was a small contingent of Royal Air Force officers and men, including families of those of higher rank. While the Americans were noisy and outgoing, the British were quiet and reserved. At times I didn't even notice their presence anymore. They stayed pretty much to themselves. In terms of economics, their impact on Fassberg was minimal, in contrast to the easy spending of the Americans. However, the air base did not close, as it had twice before, and there were still jobs remaining to be done by German workers. And that was a good sign.

Between the end of the airlift in 1949 until German sovereignty and NATO membership in 1955, British usage of Fassberg Air Base included a brief period when three squadrons of Vampire jets were moved to RAF Fassberg. Fassberg, once an aircrew training center for the Luftwaffe, later a transport hub during the Berlin airlift, now became a forward operating base for Royal Air Force fighter bombers. In 1951 Group Captain Johnnie Johnson, the highest scoring British fighter ace in World War II, assumed command of the Fassberg wing. He was an up and coming RAF officer and soon was moved to RAF Wildenrath in 1952. The de Havilland Vampire had replaced the Gloster Meteor, the first British jet developed in the later stages of World War II. The Vampire was a twin-boom aircraft, similar in looks to Kelly Johnson's P-38, only it was a jet fighter while the P-38 was conventionally powered. The Vampire evolved into the more capable Venom fighter bomber, and in the summer of 1953 the Venom replaced the Vampire in Number 14, 98, and 118 Squadrons at RAF Fassberg. RAF Celle, at the time, also transitioned its three squadrons to the Venom. The Venom didn't stay all that long in Fassberg. In 1955 the Fassberg RAF squadrons upgraded again, this time to the Hawker Hunter. This aircraft, with a new type of engine, and near supersonic speed when at its best, would serve in the RAF in many roles for years to come. However, its stay at RAF Fassberg was to be very short. In March 1956 the Bundeswehr began to form its first units, including a new beginning for the West German air force, the resurrected Luft-

RAF Gloster Meteors, the first British jet fighter produced in World War II, only saw limited wartime action. The Meteor, with a very different design concept from the German Me 262 that used podded engines hung under its wings, became the design standard of the future. The Meteors were replaced by de Havilland Vampires, which in turn was replaced by the de Havilland Venom, an upgraded version of the Vampire. Photo courtesy of Albert S. Tucker.

A Cold War formation of NATO reconnaissance aircraft, around 1970. Canadian F-104, German F-104, US RF-4, British Hawker Hunter, a Belgian RF-84, and a Dutch RF-104. Photo provided by the author.

Sign near the Fassberg Air Base main gate identifying the principal purpose of the air base at the time—technical training. Photo provided by the author.

waffe. The majority of British soldiers and families left Fassberg early that December of 1956, leaving behind only a small contingent which dealt with issues related to the handover of the air base to its new occupants, the German air force. That small group of RAF officers and men left on March 29, 1957, ending twelve years of occupation and use of Fassberg by British and American flying units.

The first use of Fassberg Air Base by the Germans was somewhat out of character, hosting the Offiziersschule der Luftwaffe, their officer training school, an important institution, of course, in a newly formed, democratic air force. However, Fassberg, in the past, had always been an aircrew training center, an important part of the Berlin airlift, in other words, a flying base. The school only stayed in Fassberg for a brief two years then, in 1958, moved to Neubiberg Air Base, a former airfield used by American transport units. Then Fassberg returned to its former self, becoming the Technische Schule der Luftwaffe, its technical training center.

Fassberg Air Base main gate on the *Grosse Horststrasse* after reverting back to the Luftwaffe in 1956. Over the years and under varying circumstances this gatehouse had been occupied by men wearing German, British, and American uniforms. Photo provided by the author.

Technical training at Fassberg encompassed everything from truck maintenance to aircraft maintenance, at all levels of expertise, from apprentice to master technician. To that end the school had various aircraft and vehicles used by the Bundeswehr available for its training purposes, stored in two of the numerous aircraft hangars that Fassberg Air Base was blessed with. When the officers' training school moved to Neubiberg that October, a fighter-bomber wing of F-84F aircraft took its place, Jabo-Geschwader 34. Fassberg again experienced real aircraft noise, a welcome sign for the civilians who worked at the air base. Aircraft noise meant jobs, and a secure future for the town of Fassberg. It quickly became evident that the existing runways were inadequate, so the principal concrete runway was extended to three thousand meters, over nine thousand feet, a runway that could accommodate every NATO aircraft flying at the time.

This runway extension would be important for future operations not yet anticipated. Jabo-Geschwader 34, like the officer training school before it, moved out in April of 1959, after just six short months, to Memmingen, Bavaria. From 1973 to 1975 I served two years as an exchange officer at the Luftwaffe's Generalstabslehrgang in Hamburg-Blankenese. One of my classmates, then Lieutenant Colonel, later Major General Horst Lemke, would in 1989 serve as the Memmingen wing commander flying F-104G Starfighters.

In addition, in 1958, the Luftwaffe chose to move its helicopter pilot training program to Fassberg, providing training for not just Luftwaffe pilots, but for the army and navy as well. That lasted for about fifteen years into the early 1970s, at which time the German army's Transport Helicopter Regiment 10, flying Bell UH-1Ds, became the principal occupant of the air base—and with that change Fassberg became a *Heeresflugplatz*, an army airfield. Fassberg Air Base, to this day, accommodates both army and air force units. During a visit in 2002 I just happened to be there when one of their Bell UH-1s returned from a training flight, and I had the opportunity to exchange a few friendly words with the two pilots.

In many ways Fassberg Air Base has changed little, and anyone who served there years ago would easily find his way around. The buildings on the air base proper are largely under *Denkmalschutz*, historical preservation, meaning that structural changes require government approval, which isn't easy to come by. By the time of my visit the town had expanded considerably and there no longer was any fear of the airfield being shut down. In 1936, when Fassberg was created, the number of town residents was something around 700, by the time of the airlift in 1948 that number had reportedly expanded to around 2,700. By 1970 the number of Fassberg residents had doubled to around 5,500, and the town keeps on growing and evolving, reaching 6,136 residents in January of 2019. A change came in the 1980s, when Fassberg Air Base again served a potential wartime role. Not an offensive role by any measure, but as the occasional host of

Helicopters of the Fassberg multiservice helicopter training school. An American UH-1D Huey and a former Russian-built East German air force Mi-8. Photo provided by the author.

Allied fighter bombers training to assure the protection of rail and road traffic between West Germany and Berlin should the Soviets again choose to interfere.

13

Exercise Treaty

19 September 1950. The Council of Foreign Ministers declares the Allied Governments will treat any attack upon the German Federal Republic or upon West Berlin as an attack upon themselves.
—*The American Military Occupation of Germany 1945–1953*

Fassberg was a border town, only thirty kilometers from the inner German border between East Germany, the Deutsche Demokratische Republik (DDR), and West Germany, the Federal Republic of Germany (FRG); or what once was the border between the American and British zones and the Russian zone of occupation. The border, although patrolled by Russian troops and by East German police working for the Russians, initially was a relatively open border. Easy to cross, as I did in 1946 with my mother and father. Soviet rule over its zone of occupation and countries under its control, such as Poland, Hungary, Czechoslovakia, and others, was harsh. Retribution was the first order of business after war's end; authorities sought to punish and eliminate all who were suspect of not being loyal Communists or those having transgressions, however minor, reported against them. Citizens feared the nighttime knock on the door and often disappeared never to be seen again. By 1950 a mass exodus from East to the West was well underway, leading the Rus-

The wall ran right in front of the Brandenburg Gate, flying the East German flag. The Berlin of the East was a decrepit and dismal place, dark at night, with few cars driving its streets. Much war damage remained. The West was exemplified by the Kurfuerstendam, an upscale shopping street in Berlin, which was a scene of light and traffic jams, of stores filled with luxury goods—a window to the West at its best. The next photograph shows another view of the wall after its completion, looking into East Berlin, showing the death strip with barriers to prevent escapes. Photo provided by the author.

sians to take measures to put a stop to it in 1952. The inner German border was first secured by barbed wire only, and occasional patrols, then augmented by antipersonnel mines and other obstacles, making escape difficult and life-threatening.

The only remaining safe escape route was through Berlin. All one had to do was get there and jump on the S-Bahn, the elevated train that ran through all sectors of Berlin, and get off at a station in one of the Western sectors and apply for refugee status. After all the paperwork was done, refugees were put on a plane and flown out to the West. By 1961 nearly 20 percent of the East German population had defected to the West. Not only that, the defectors were the best and the brightest—engineers, doctors, university professors, teachers, and technicians—the people who made things work and kept things running. It was a brain drain that condemned the DDR to the level of an agricultural society with little or no technical and innovative capacity. Walter Ulbricht, with numerous meaningless titles, but the chief decision maker of the SED (Socialistische Einheitspartei Deutschland), decided to put a stop to it. The solution he came up with was the Berlin Wall, a wall that would run through and around the city isolating the Western Sectors from the Eastern Sector. Ulbricht had his army stockpile enough barbed wire to string a fence along the nearly one hundred miles of border between West Berlin and East Berlin and adjacent East Germany, as well as building materials to start the construction of a wall that would take the place of the barbed wire. This wall in future years was adjacent to a death strip from which all vegetation was removed, so movement could easily be detected. The strip was lit at night and observation towers allowed guards to fire at anyone who dared to enter this zone of death. On Sunday, August 13, 1961, the door slammed shut. The East Germans closed the border to West Berlin.

Soviet Premier Nikita Khrushchev had turned over control of East Berlin to the East German state, the DDR. The DDR was neither democratic nor a republic, but it had Russian backing and the wall

Checkpoint Charlie in later years. I frequently crossed over into East Berlin in the early 1980s through Checkpoint Charlie on official Air Force business. If one needed a reminder of the differences between East and West, driving through East Berlin provided that opportunity in spades. The large structure in the distance in the middle of the road was the Russian/East German entry point, and everyone who entered was photographed from the top of that tower. Photo provided by the author.

went up. The wall was an unmistakable challenge to the West, even if it was built to keep the DDR alive. And later in August President Kennedy ordered the National Guard and Reserves to active duty resulting in a massive transfer of American air power to Europe. By October 27, 1961, things came close to getting out of hand. Russian and American tanks faced each other at Check Point Charlie, one of the crossings into and out of East Berlin.

The confrontation lasted seventeen hours, before both sides backed down. However, the wall remained, and the Western Allies made no further efforts to remove it. It would come down thirty years later, on November 9, 1989, when the DDR crumbled. The Soviet Union followed suit in December 1991, and with that the Cold War ended.

A Bentwaters A-10 of the 509th Tactical Fighter Squadron at Zaragoza Air Base, Spain, preparing to load a rack of five-hundred-pound Mk 82 Snake Eye practice bombs for a training run later that day at the Zaragoza bombing range. The 509th had the Exercise Treaty assignment. Photo provided by the author.

Although at this time in 1961 the Soviets and East Germans did not in any significant way hinder the flow of traffic between West Germany and Berlin, the Checkpoint Charlie confrontation pointed out all too clearly that things could deteriorate very quickly. In addition it pointed to structural and command and control deficiencies and a lack of conventional combat power within NATO and in Berlin, which after all was still an occupied city. In response, the United States combined all of its military forces in Berlin under the Berlin Brigade, moved in more armor, and increased conventional combat power based in West Germany. The United States, France, and Great Britain—the three Western occupying powers of Berlin—decided to develop a quick reaction capability, just in case. And with that decision little old Fassberg again became a player—this time around to maintain the peace rather than be part of starting a war.

In 1973 to 1975 I served as an exchange officer with the German air force in Hamburg. My young son Charles was eleven years old in 1973.

He and his sister Shelley, eight, attended the International School in Hamburg, and we had frequent occasions to visit Fassberg, where I had attended school as a refugee from Silesia. In 1985 I retired from the United States Air Force, but before doing so I swore in my son at Ohio State University, in Columbus, as a Second Lieutenant in the United States Air Force. It was a great moment for us both. Charles soon headed off to Euro/NATO pilot training at Wichita Falls, Texas, flying with British, Dutch, Danish, German, and other NATO officers in pilot training. The following year he found himself at Davis-Monthan Air Force Base, Arizona, training in the fearsome A-10 Warthog—an aircraft with a big gun specifically developed for close air support and killing tanks. In 1987 he arrived at the 509th Tactical Fighter squadron, 81st Tactical Fighter Wing, RAF Bentwaters, United Kingdom. The Wing had six squadrons of A-10 aircraft, eighteen aircraft per squadron, and it was the 509th that was assigned a unique role in the defense of Berlin, over and above its NATO commitments.

Should the Soviets or East Germans ever again attempt to limit or in any way interfere with Allied surface traffic to and from Berlin, the 509th would be called out to provide close air support for a US, British, and French army combat team tasked to deal with whatever obstacles the East put in their way to Berlin. In addition, a Wild Weasel squadron from the 52nd Tactical Fighter Wing at Spangdahlem Air Base was slated to provide the essential SAM suppression capability. On the French side a squadron of Mirage V aircraft based at Colmar, France, provided interdiction capability, as did a squadron of British Jaguars. British Harriers augmented the A-10 capability in the close air support role. All of this was outside the conventional NATO structure because the city of Berlin was still an occupied city, occupied by the United States, Britain, and France and therefore those three nations provided the necessary muscle, of course, with NATO's power potential at their back. In addition the German air force provided the airfield and necessary support for the exercises and potential force employment.

The 480th Tactical Fighter Squadron, which provided the SAM killing capability, flew both F-16 and F-4G aircraft. The F-4G was the hunter, finding the missile site, the F-16 was the killer which would take out the site. It was a true team effort. In the background behind the F-16 are two British Jaguars which participated in Exercise Treaty. Photo courtesy of Charles W. Samuel.

A Spangdahlem 52nd Tactical Fighter Wing F-4G upon arrival at Fassberg Air Base for Exercise Treaty. All air and maintenance crews thoroughly enjoyed the comradery that evolved during this combined exercise. All year long the crews were looking forward to the next event. Photo courtesy of Charles W. Samuel.

A French Mirage V on a practice run during Exercise Treaty. Each squadron usually sent four to five aircraft for this exercise which lasted about five days. There was a morning and an afternoon launch of at least sixteen aircraft on a preplanned exercise scenario. Photo courtesy of Charles W. Samuel.

The American, French, British, and German flags along the taxiway are at half-mast as an A-10 taxis by to get ready for launch. Two days earlier, on August 28, 1988, the Italian Air Force Demonstration team, flying at Ramstein Air Base, experienced a tragic midair collision resulting in seventy fatalities, including sixty-seven spectators, and the loss of three aircraft. Photo courtesy of Charles W. Samuel.

The Gundlach flower shop in 1989. Today Eberhard's daughter Petra is running things and her shop is called Kreative Floristik zu Jedem Anlass, Creative Floristics for Every Occasion. Photo courtesy of Charles W. Samuel.

The airfield selected for this effort was Fassberg. Once a year British, French, and American aircraft would arrive at Fassberg under the code name Exercise Treaty and would hone their skills to work as a team should the requirement ever arise for them to protect an Allied combat team trying to make its way to Berlin.

Exercise Treaty was an annual exercise in which my son Charles participated in 1987, 1988, and 1989. In November of 1989 the Berlin Wall came down, and there was no further need to continue this exercise. My son knew Fassberg well from his early days as a youngster when I was stationed in Germany, and we made frequent visits there, especially in August when the heath was in bloom. And of course we went to visit our friends, such as Eberhard Gundlach with whom I attended school in Fassberg.

Getting the flyers from four nations together was not all work, but provided the opportunity for enjoyable companionship, cement-

The German night was the only rather formal event. All the other nights were much more informal. Photo courtesy of Charles W. Samuel.

French night participants enjoying red wine and companionship. Swapping flight suits was a tradition during this exercise in the spirit of Tripartite cooperation. They worked hard during the day and let off steam at night. It's what airmen do. Photo courtesy of Charles W. Samuel.

ing bonds between longtime allies. The exercise lasted about a week, and during that time period they found time to have four major social functions, always in the evenings, at the *Offiziersheim* at the Fassberg Flugplatz. There was a German night, the big opening night; then a French night event, a British night, and the American night at the very end. Of course the hosts, the German air force, put on the more formal event, it being the welcoming event of the exercise. As the week progressed the events became less and less formal. During the British night, of course, they served fish and chips and drank warm British beer. The French, not to be outdone, flew in their wine from Colmar, French wine country, and made for an upscale evening—lots of hangovers the next day. And the Americans came up with their world famous frozen Margueritas—the biggest problem was getting enough ice for the popular drink. Fassberg only had two small ice machines—that was it. What to do now? No ice, no Margueritas. One of the F-4G pilots from the 52nd Tactical Fighter Wing suddenly recalled a maintenance issue that had to be resolved immediately before the next day's launch, an issue that could only be resolved at his home base, Spangdahlem, in the Eifel mountains. Before you could say "pull the chocks," that F-4G was airborne and arrived at Spang, as the base was normally referred to, within the hour. Two waiting wing pods filled with ice were uploaded, and forty-five minutes later Fassberg had all the Marguerita ice needed for a great evening of bonding. In peace and war there are situations not planned for needing prompt and positive resolution—this was such a situation which was resolved in an appropriate and timely manner. After all, American prestige was on the line.

Exercise Treaty was serious business and my son Charles thoroughly enjoyed the opportunity to fly with French and British aviators. A truly bonding experience. Charles had a painting commissioned by the renowned aviation artist Geoff Pleasance of four Allied aircraft flying in formation in the Fassberg area during Exercise Treaty. Since Charles was an A-10 pilot, it is no surprise that the

A-10 is leading the four-ship of a French Mirage, British Jaguar, and British Harrier.

Fassberg, a town and air base created for war, in years to come would be the location for peace-saving efforts such as the Berlin air-lift and Exercise Treaty. Air base and town are closely linked to this day. As for myself, Fassberg always will be an important way station in my life, a town where my father served, a town where I grew up in difficult times, a town where my son served in the cause of peace. God bless this little unpretentious town and may it never again have to experience the scourge of war.

POSTSCRIPT

I don't recall what dreams I may have had for my future as a boy of ten, but it didn't include war as I experienced it. If death was portrayed as something magic in the fairy tales I read, with a soul looking like a feather escaping a body when a young maiden surrendered her life, the reality was beyond ugly. From one day to the next I suddenly passed from a sheltered childhood, with a nice home and friends and all the things that go with it, to the sudden loss of everything that anchored my life. In the closing days of World War II, running for safety with a fleeing German army unit took me into the midst of combat and the ugliness of death. There was no beauty about the dead, no souls calmly escaping their bodies; there was only torn flesh, dead eyes, the smell of war which would never leave my memory. I was lucky. I survived. I had a wonderful mother who somehow managed to get her children through it all. A little over a year after the guns stopped firing I found myself in a refugee camp in a strange place adjacent to the airfield and a town called Fassberg, situated in the Lueneburg Heath, a barren landscape filled with the detritus of war. I was at a new beginning, I knew that. But where my future path of life would lead, I had no idea.

Life in a refugee camp was all about the basics—shelter, warmth, food of whatever kind, clean water, and anything to wear to stay warm. Every day was a struggle for survival. But I was lucky again. The nearby town of Fassberg had survived war pretty much unscathed, and there I found some normalcy of life, including the ability to con-

Pass issued to my father by the US Army on May 29, 1945, the day he arrived at the POW camp near Colmar, France. Strangely, years later, the French fighter squadron that participated in Exercise Treaty was based in Colmar. Photo provided by the author.

tinue my education, which had pretty much come to a halt in January 1945. To my great surprise, since war's end, the outside world had changed significantly, and suddenly I found myself witnessing an unprecedented airlift flown by American and British airmen, former enemies, to save the city of Berlin. A city where I lived for a period of time to experience the terror of massive bombing raids. Now it seemed that the same people who once terrified me in my makeshift shelter in Berlin were willing to die to save the city I once called home. I had no heroes in those days of fear and deprivation, but suddenly, while viewing the crash site of an American transport, I wanted to be like them, be like people who could forgive and had empathy and compassion for a former enemy. Of course I didn't know anything about the political aims of the Americans and the

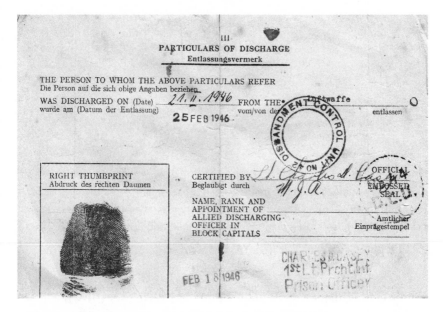

My father's official discharge paper from the Luftwaffe and release as a prisoner of war. Signed by First Lieutenant Charles D. Casey, Prison Officer, 42nd Disbandment Control Unit, United States Army. Photo provided by the author.

British in 1948, all I knew was that they were saving me from again having to live under Russian occupation.

The large transports flying coal to Berlin from the Fassberg airfield, adjacent to the camp I called home, was a reassuring sound for this young boy. It meant, or I thought it meant, freedom. Freedom to me was to live in a place where there was no knock on the door at night by men with hard eyes who would take you away never to be seen again. Freedom to me meant being able to learn things I wanted to learn and being able to express myself without worrying that something bad might happen as a result of what I said. Freedom was that I could go wherever without having to get permission, a place where people could have fun, laugh, and do things people do without anyone telling them that it was right or wrong. The American soldiers of the Berlin airlift seemed like that. They knew how to laugh, were approachable and always ready with a candy bar or a stick of chewing

A picture of a Mirage V from the French Colmar squadron presented to the German air force hosts at Fassberg Air Base after Exercise Treaty 1985. My son Charles would participate during the last three years in Treaty 1987, 1988, and 1989 flying the A-10. Photo courtesy of Charles W. Samuel.

gum. So as a thirteen-year-old I wanted to be like them, live in a place like where they came from, although I had no real idea what that place might be like. And maybe, just maybe, I thought, if miracles could happen, I would love to wear their uniform and fly with them. I knew that would never come about; but it was a dream I had, my dream.

The reason my family ended up near Fassberg, the town and the airfield, was because Fassberg was my father's last assignment in the Luftwaffe. His unit was ordered to head south toward Bavaria as the British army approached, and he was captured by Patton's troops and put in a POW camp in Alsace-Lorraine, France.

On February 21, 1946, Willie was formally discharged from the Luftwaffe by an American Disbandment Control Unit and released as a POW on February 25, 1946. POWs were released to their former home addresses, which in my father's case would have been Sagan, now occupied by the Russians and part of the territory ceded to Poland under the Yalta agreement. He had no intention of going there, so he claimed Oberohe, a small village near Fassberg, as his home and was discharged to that destination.

My father and mother got a divorce soon after Willie had reunited us all. During the airlift Hedy met Master Sergeant Leo

Ferguson, and the two got married in 1950 in Fuerstenfeldbruck, Bavaria. In February 1951 I accompanied Hedy and Leo to Denver, Colorado. Two years later I graduated from East High School in Denver, and in 1960 I graduated from the University of Colorado in Boulder, Colorado, and was commissioned a second lieutenant in the United States Air Force. That impossible dream I had as a thirteen-year-old for some unexplainable reason came true for me. In my second year of flight training I flew in some of the C-54 transports which had flown coal from Fassberg and Celle—it was like a homecoming for me. I recall walking around each of the aircraft and giving them an affectionate pat in tribute to their Berlin airlift service. It was very personal for me—they were my saviors. And sure enough in time I flew with men who had flown coal and food from Fassberg, Celle, Frankfurt, and Wiesbaden to Berlin. I then was stationed with the US Air Force in Germany, getting my flying time with the 36th Tactical Fighter Wing at Bitburg Air Base, later with the 52nd Tactical Fighter Wing at nearby Spangdahlem Air Base, both bases in the Eifel mountains near Wittlich. My subsequent assignment was as an exchange officer with the German air force in Hamburg, not very far from Fassberg, where I attended the 15th Generalstabslehrgang der Luftwaffe and made many new friends serving in the new Luftwaffe.

I recall my first visit "home," to where I grew up as a young teenager, Fassberg. My young son Charles age eleven was along. I met old school friends which led to many return visits to Fassberg while I was stationed in Germany and in subsequent years. What I had never anticipated was that my young son would someday fly his A-10 attack aircraft out of Fassberg Air Base, the same place where his grandfather once was stationed during the war years and where I grew up as a teenager.

Life has its ironies and twists and turns. I would have never thought that the small town of Fassberg and its air base would become such an important and lasting part of my family's life.

My dear stepfather, Leo Ferguson, retired from the Air Force soon after we arrived in the United States in 1951. He continued to work at Lowry Air Force Base in Denver as a logistician. He died all too young, in his early sixties of lung cancer. The cigarettes he so dearly loved to smoke exacted the ultimate penalty. He and Hedy are buried in Logan National Cemetery in Denver, Colorado.

GLOSSARY

Bundeswehr	German Armed Forces—Current
DDR	Deutsche Demokratische Republik
EATS	European Air Transport Service
Fluechtling	Refugee
Flugplatz	Military airfield
FRG	Federal Republic of Germany
GCA	Ground control approach radar
Gasthaus	Country inn, small hotel and restaurant
GCLO	German Civilian Labor Organization
JG	Jagdgeschwader/Fighter Wing
KG	Kampfgeschwader/Combat Wing
Luftwaffe	German air force
NAAFE	Navy Army Air Force Exchange (British)
NATO	North Atlantic Treaty Organization
Oberleutnant	First Lieutenant
Partei	Nazi party
PX	Post exchange (US)
RAF	Royal Air Force
SAC	Strategic Air Command
SAM	Surface to Air Missile
Staffel	German for squadron
TDY	Temporary duty
USAFE	United States Air Forces Europe

USSTAF	United States Strategic Air Forces, became USAFE in 1945
Volkssturm	Militia—of the very young and very old
Waffen-SS	The combat arm of Hitler's army that existed alongside the regular German army
Wehrmacht	German Armed Forces—WWII

PHOTOGRAPHIC CREDITS

Fassberg C-54s waiting for their Block Time to come up so they could take off. The PSP, Pierced Steel Matting, clearly visible, was used in lieu of a hard surface runway. Photo courtesy of the Fassberg Airlift Museum.

381st BG
Berlin Airlift Veterans Association
Thomas Etherson
Fassberg Airlift Museum, Erinnerungsstaette Luftbruecke Berlin
M. Frauenheim
Joseph Gyulavics
Robert 'Moe' Hamill
Joseph Laufer

Frederick McIntosh
Samuel Myers
Charles W. Samuel
Wolfgang W. E. Samuel
Leonard Sweet
Albert S. Tucker

BIBLIOGRAPHY

The American Military Occupation of Germany 1945–1953. Headquarters, United States Army, Europe, 1953.

Berlin Airlift: A USAFE Summary. Headquarters, United States Air Forces in Europe, APO 633, 1949.

Blazek, Matthias. *Die geheime Grossbaustelle in der Heide—Fassberg und sein Fliegerhorst 1933–2013.* Stuttgart: Ibidem Verlag, 2013.

Butler, Phil. *War Prizes.* Leicester: Midland Counties Publications, 1994.

Carter, Kit C. and Robert Mueller. *The Army Air Forces in World War II, Combat Chronology 1941–1945.* Headquarters, United States Air Force, 1973.

Collier, Richard. *Bridge across the Sky: The Berlin Blockade and Airlift, 1948–1949.* New York: McGraw Hill, 1978.

Ferrell, Robert H., ed. *The Twentieth Century: An Almanac.* New York: World Almanac Publications, 1985.

Glombek, Christoph M. *Chronik der Gemeinde Fassberg.* Fassberg: Eigenverlag, 2002.

LeMay, Curtis E., with MacKinlay Kantor. *Mission with LeMay, My Story.* Garden City, NY: Doubleday, 1965.

Kruppik, Rainer, et al. *Erinnerungsstaette Luftbruecke Berlin.* Fassberg: Technische Schule der Luftwaffe, no date.

McCullough, David. *Truman.* New York: Simon and Schuster, 1992.

Miller, Roger C. *To Save a City: The Berlin Airlift 1948–1949.* College Station: Texas A&M University Press, 2000.

Reeves, Richard. *Daring Young Men: The Heroism and Triumph of the Berlin Airlift, June 1948–May 1949.* New York: Simon and Schuster, 2010.

Reitsch, Hanna. *Flying Is My Life.* New York: G. P. Putnam's Sons, 1954.

Ridgway, Matthew B. *Soldier: The Memoirs of Matthew B. Ridgway.* Westport, CT: Greenwood Press, 1974.

Samuel, Wilhelm. *Wehrpass, Fliegerschule Neuruppin*, Germany, 1937.

Samuel, Wolfgang W. E. *American Raiders: The Race to Capture the Luftwaffe's Secrets.* Jackson: University Press of Mississippi, 2004.

Samuel, Wolfgang W. E. *German Boy: A Refugee's Story.* Jackson: University Press of Mississippi, 2000.

Samuel, Wolfgang W. E. *I Always Wanted to Fly: America's Cold War Airmen.* Jackson: University Press of Mississippi, 2001.

Samuel, Wolfgang W. E. *The War of Our Childhood: Memories of World War II*. Jackson: University Press of Mississippi, 2002.

Schuffert, John H. *Airlift Laffs, Berlin Airlift*. San Antonio, TX: Veterans Association, 1999.

Smith, Jean Edward. *Lucius D. Clay: An American Life*. New York: Henry Holt, 1990.

Staerk, Hans. *Fassberg*. Fassberg: Selbstverlag des Verfassers, 1971.

INDEX

ABOUT THE AUTHOR

Courtesy Wolfgang W. E. Samuel

Wolfgang W. E. Samuel was born in Germany in 1935 and immigrated to the United States in 1951 at age sixteen with an eighth-grade education and no English language skills. Upon graduation from the University of Colorado, he was commissioned second lieutenant in the US Air Force, then flew over a hundred strategic reconnaissance missions against the Soviet Union during the Cold War. His first book *German Boy* garnered favorable reviews from the *New York Times* and numerous other outlets. He is author of eight books published by University Press of Mississippi.